Modern Guitar Anthems Red Book

Thirty songs arranged for Guitar Tablature Vocal.

Published 2002
International Music Publications Limited
Griffin house, 161 Hammersmith Road, London, W6 8BS, England

Edited by Chris Harvey
Folio design by Dominic Brookman

Contents

Blurry

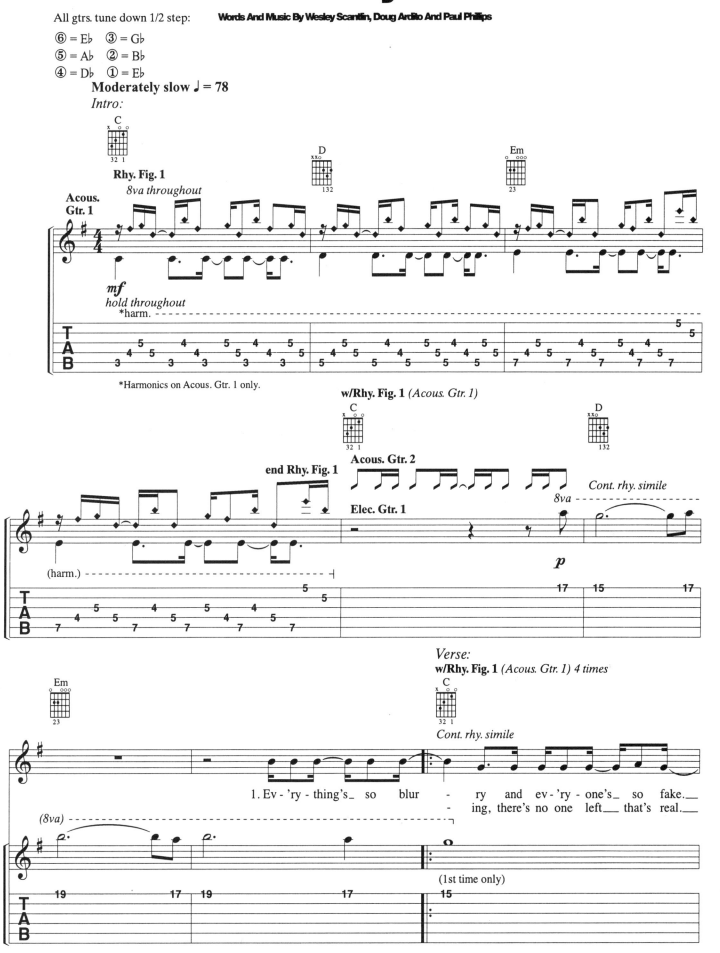

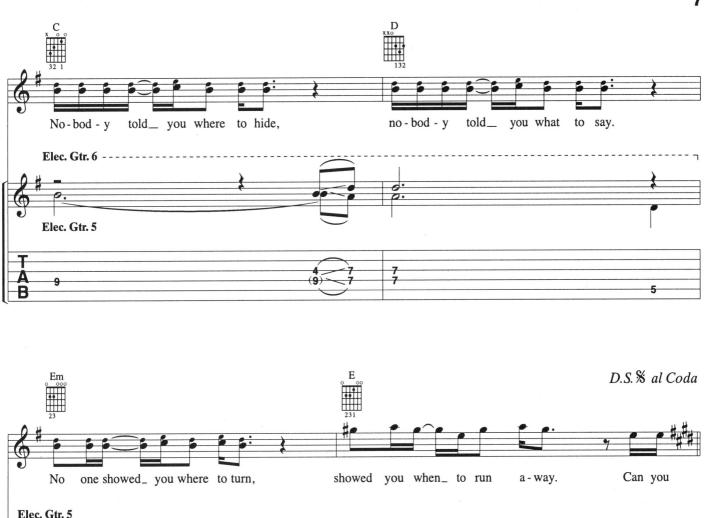

No-bod-y told_ you where to hide, no-bod-y told_ you what to say.

Elec. Gtr. 6

Elec. Gtr. 5

D.S. %. al Coda

No one showed_ you where to turn, showed you when_ to run a-way. Can you

Elec. Gtr. 5

Coda

shoved it in_ my face,_____ this pain_ you gave_ to me._____

Elec. Gtr. 5

8

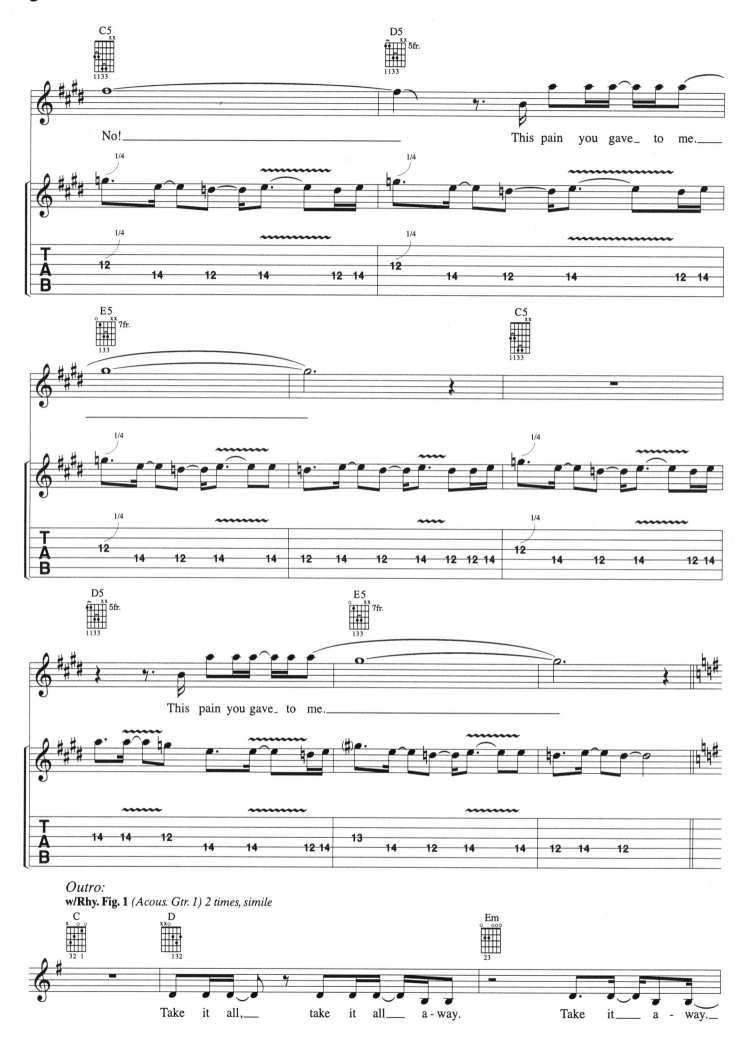

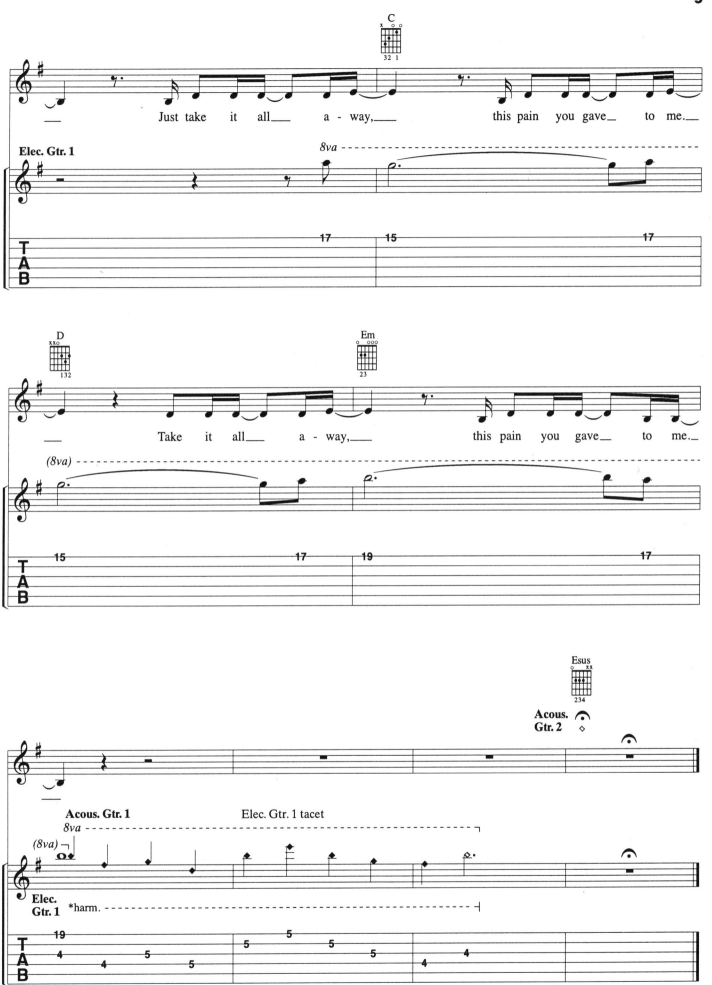

*Harmonics on Acous. Gtr. 1 only.

Between Angels & Insects

Words And Music By Tobin Esperance, Jerry Horton Jr, Jacoby Shaddix And David Buckner

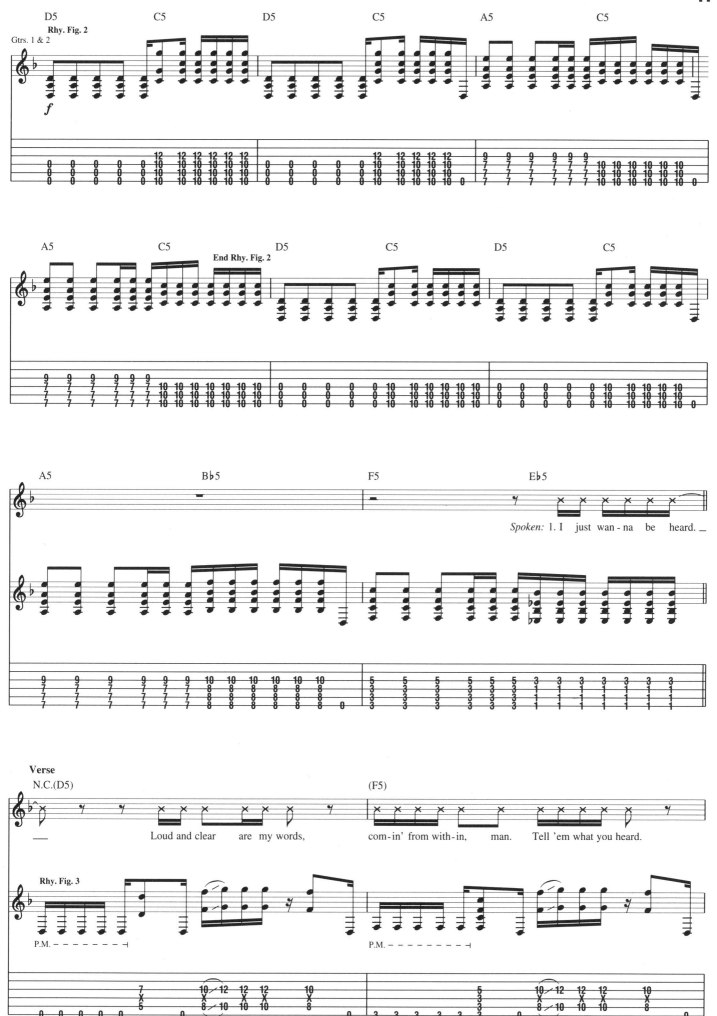

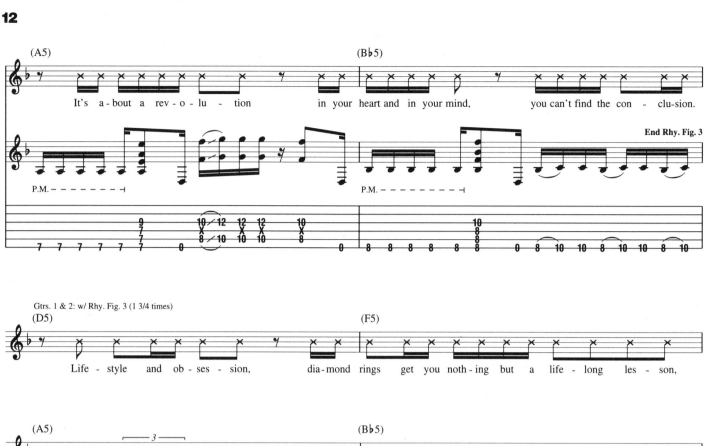

(A5) ... It's a-bout a rev-o-lu-tion in your heart and in your mind, you can't find the con-clu-sion. (Bb5) ... End Rhy. Fig. 3

Gtrs. 1 & 2: w/ Rhy. Fig. 3 (1 3/4 times)

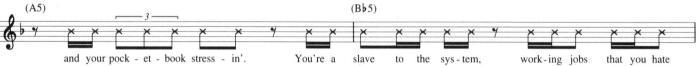

(D5) Life-style and ob-ses-sion, (F5) dia-mond rings get you noth-ing but a life-long les-son,

(A5) and your pock-et-book stress-in'. You're a slave to the sys-tem, (Bb5) work-ing jobs that you hate

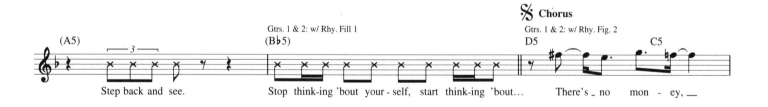

(D5) for that shit you don't need. It's too bad (F5) the world is based on greed.

𝄋 Chorus

Gtrs. 1 & 2: w/ Rhy. Fill 1

Gtrs. 1 & 2: w/ Rhy. Fig. 2

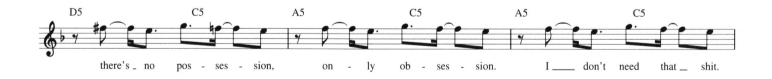

(A5) Step back and see. (Bb5) Stop think-ing 'bout your-self, start think-ing 'bout... D5 C5 There's __ no mon-ey, __

D5 C5 A5 C5 A5 C5
there's __ no pos-ses-sion, on-ly ob-ses-sion. I __ don't need that __ shit.

Rhy. Fill 1
Gtrs. 1 & 2

P.M. - - - - - - - -

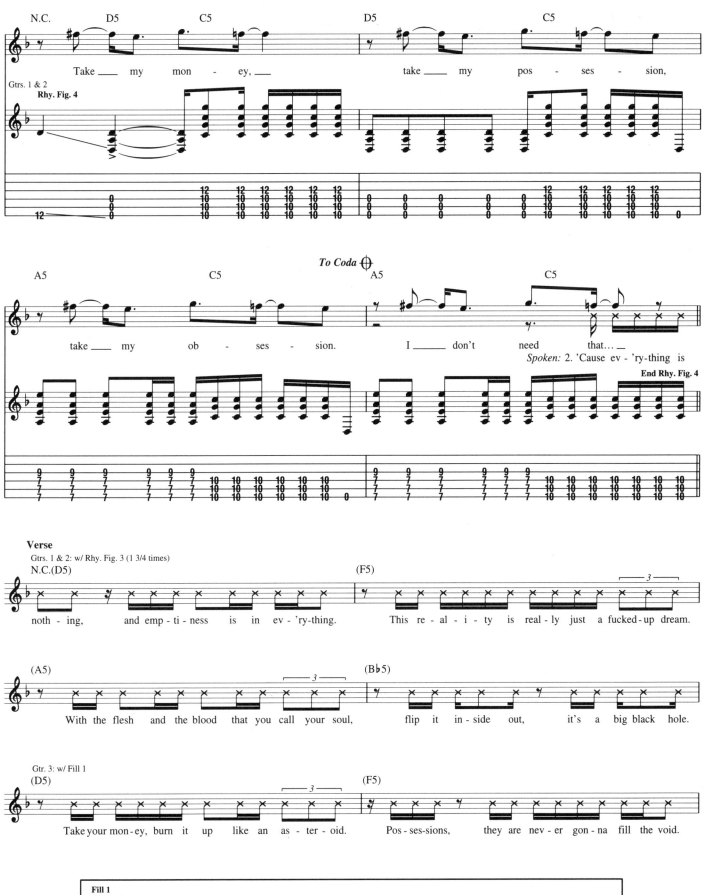

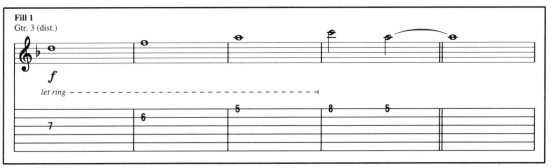

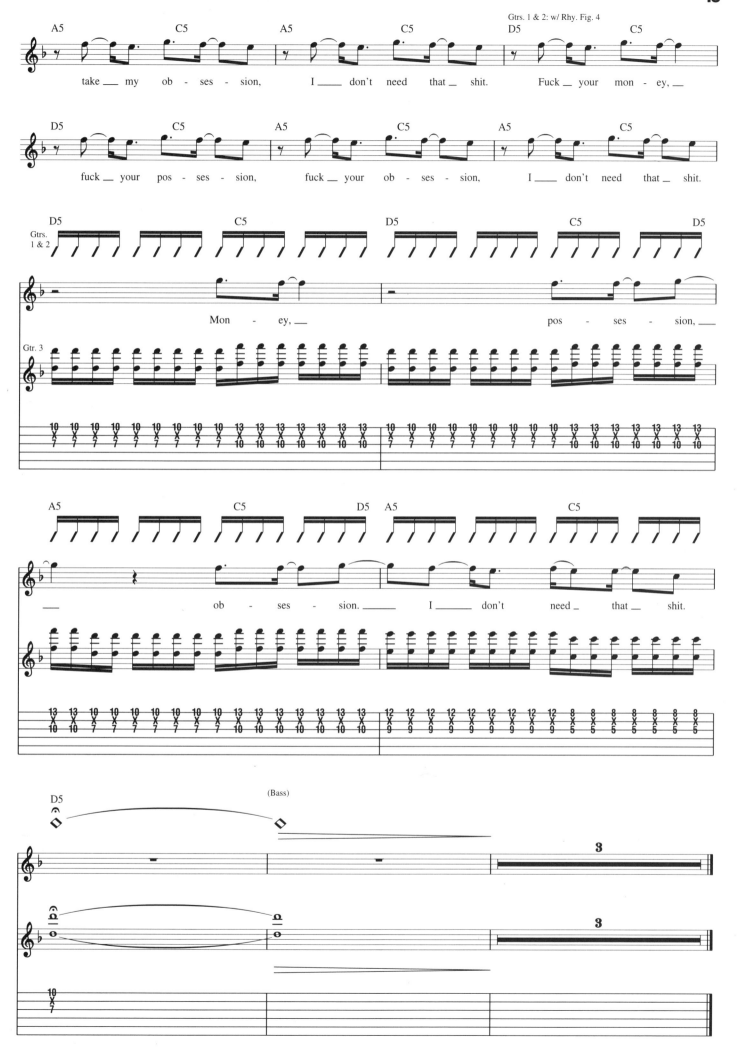

Broken Home

Words And Music By Tobin Esperance, Jerry Horton Jr., Jacoby Shaddix And David Buckner

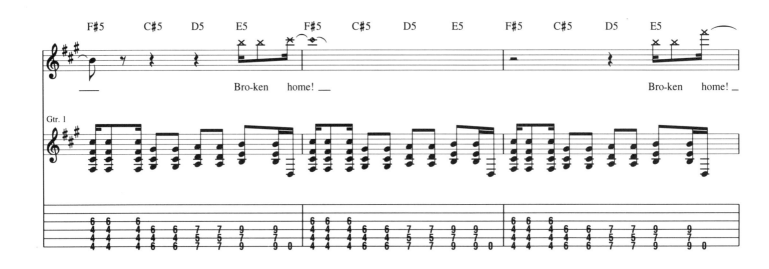

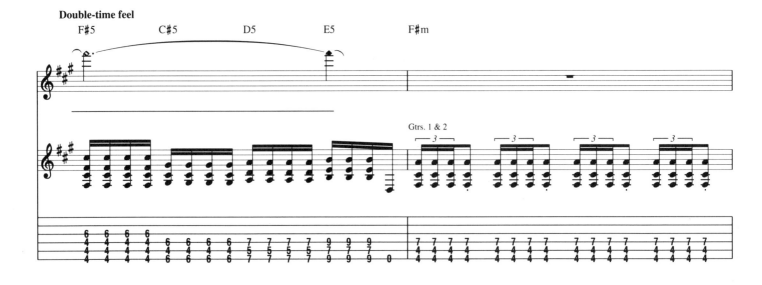

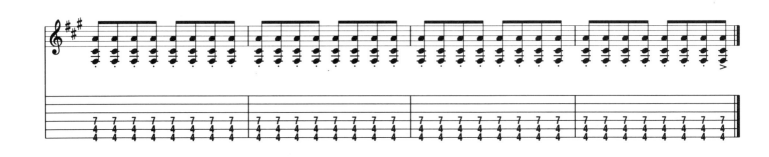

Chop Suey

Words And Music By Daron Malakian And Serj Tankian

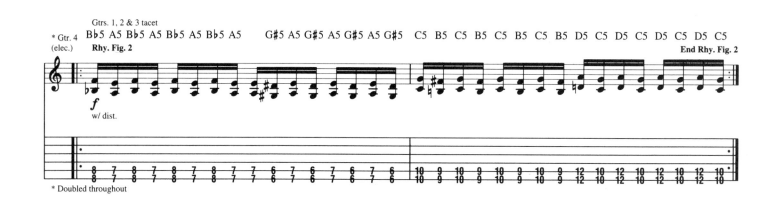

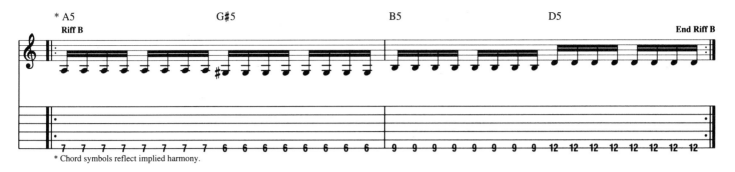

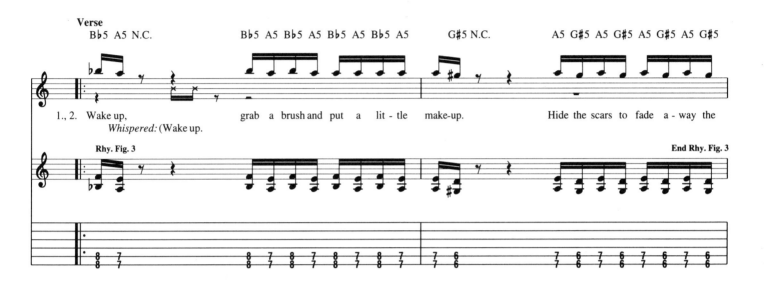

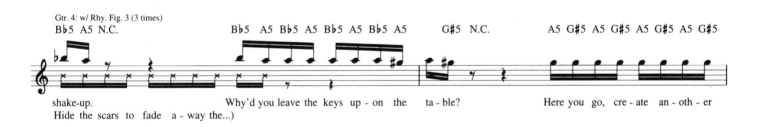

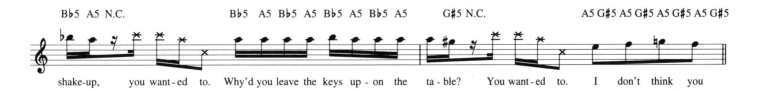

24

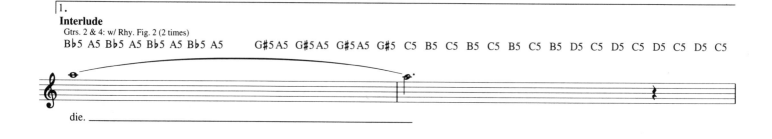

Bb5 A5 Bb5 A5 Bb5 A5 Bb5 A5   G#5 A5 G#5 A5 G#5 A5 G#5   C5 B5 C5 B5 C5 B5 C5 B5   D5 C5 D5 C5 D5 C5 D5 C5

Bb5 A5 Bb5 A5 Bb5 A5 Bb5 A5 Bb5 A5 Bb5 A5 Bb5 A5 Bb5 A5   Am

2.
Gtr. 3: w/ Riff A (1 3/4 times)
Gtr. 5: w/ Riff C2 (1 1/4 times)

Rah! _____   die

Gtrs. 2 & 4

P.M. - - - - - - - - - - - - - - - - -

Bm/A   G/A   F/A   Am

in _____ my __   self - right-eous su - i - cide. _____

P.M. -┘   *let ring* - - - - - - - - - -

Bm/A   G/A   F

I _____   cry __   when an - gels _ de - serve to die.

Gtr. 2   Gtr. 3
Gtr. 2
divisi

let ring - - - - - - - - - - -

Gtr. 5

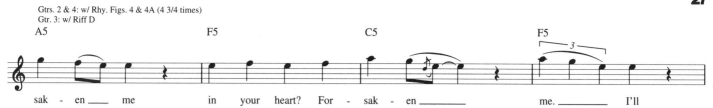

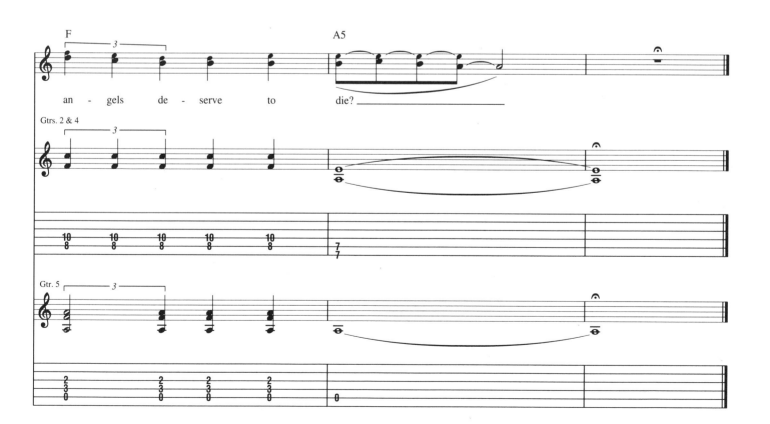

Control

Words And Music By Wesley Scantlin And Brad Stewart

All gtrs. tune down 1/2 step
w/Drop D tuning:
⑥ = D♭ ③ = G♭
⑤ = A♭ ②ᵇ = B♭
④ = D♭ ① = E♭

Moderately ♩ = 80
Intro:

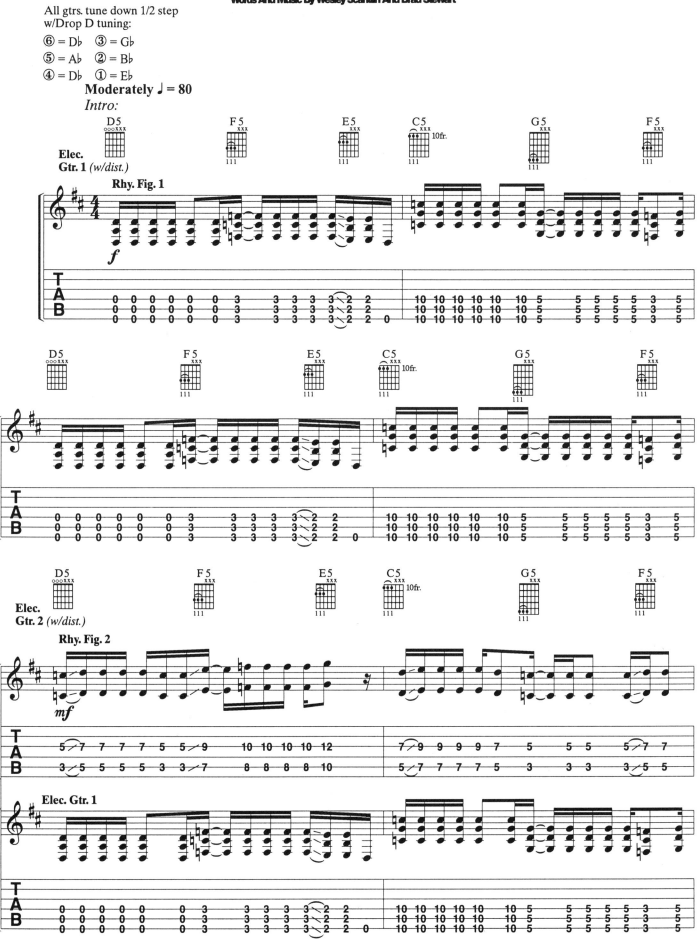

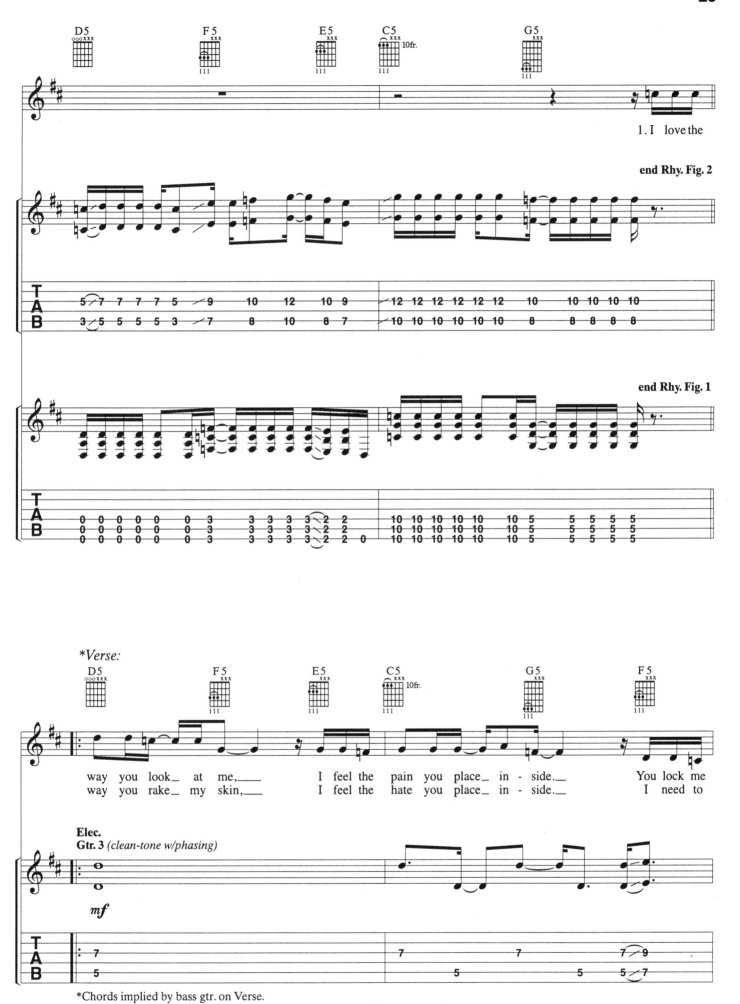

*Chords implied by bass gtr. on Verse.

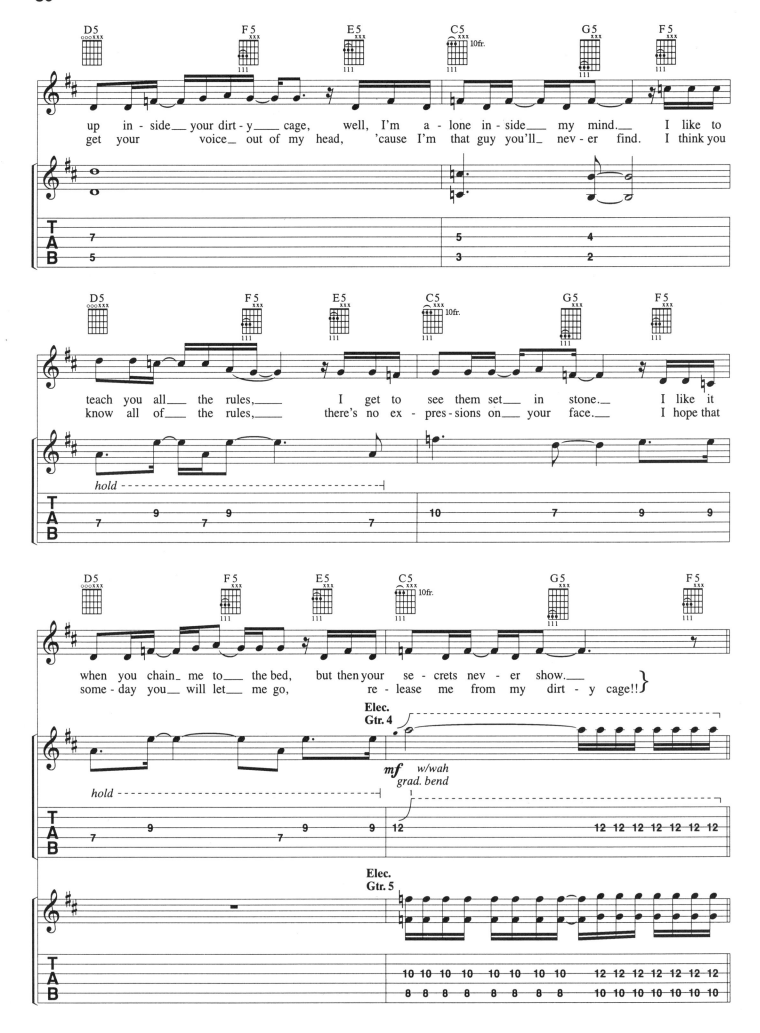

Chorus:
w/Rhy. Fig. 1 *(Elec. Gtr. 1)*

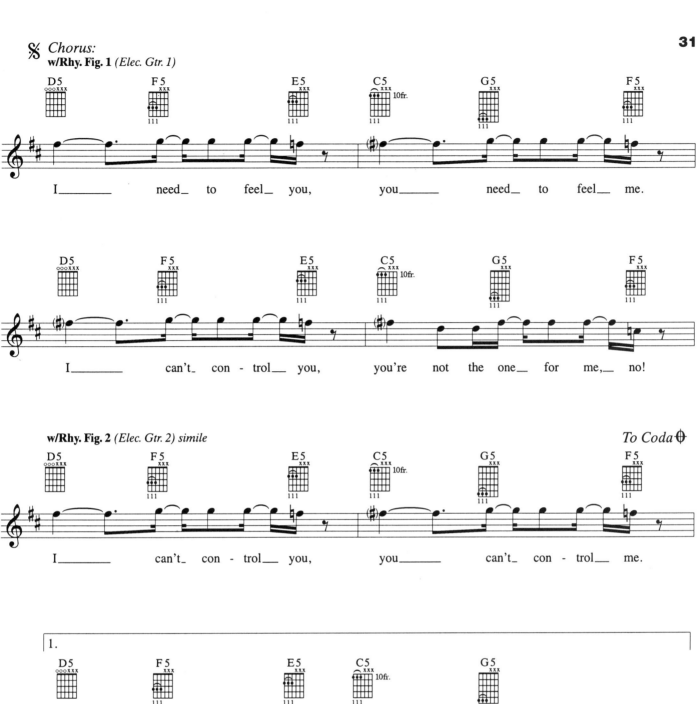

I_____ need_ to feel_ you, you_____ need_ to feel__ me.

I_____ can't_ con - trol__ you, you're not the one__ for me,__ no!

w/Rhy. Fig. 2 *(Elec. Gtr. 2) simile*

To Coda ⊕

I_____ can't_ con - trol__ you, you_____ can't_ con - trol__ me.

1.

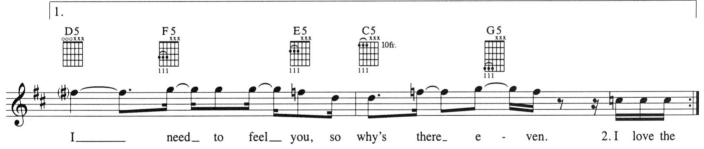

I_____ need_ to feel_ you, so why's there_ e - ven. 2. I love the

2.3.

w/Rhy. Fig. 1 *(Elec. Gtr. 1) 1st 2 meas. only*

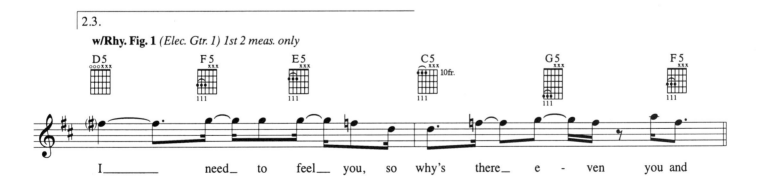

I_____ need_ to feel__ you, so why's there__ e - ven you and

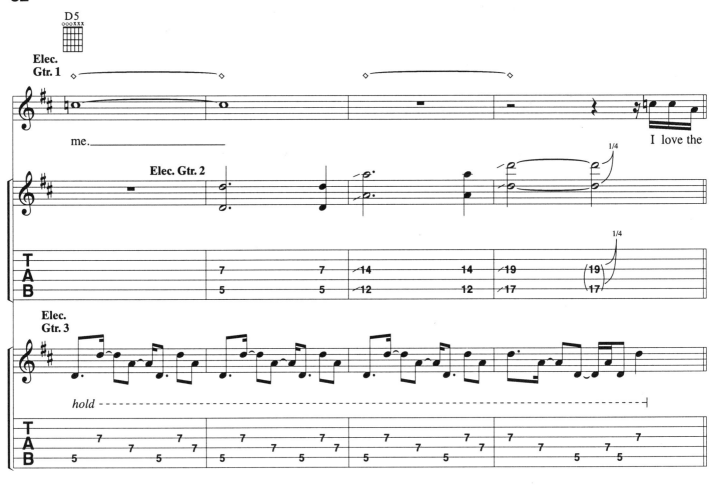

Bridge:

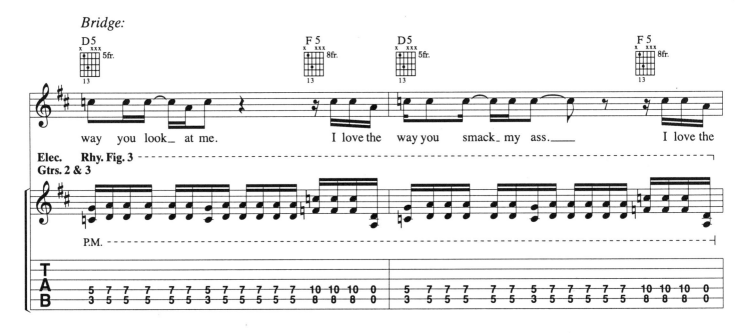

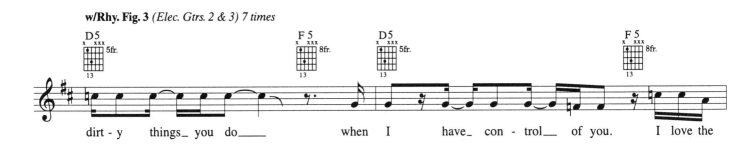

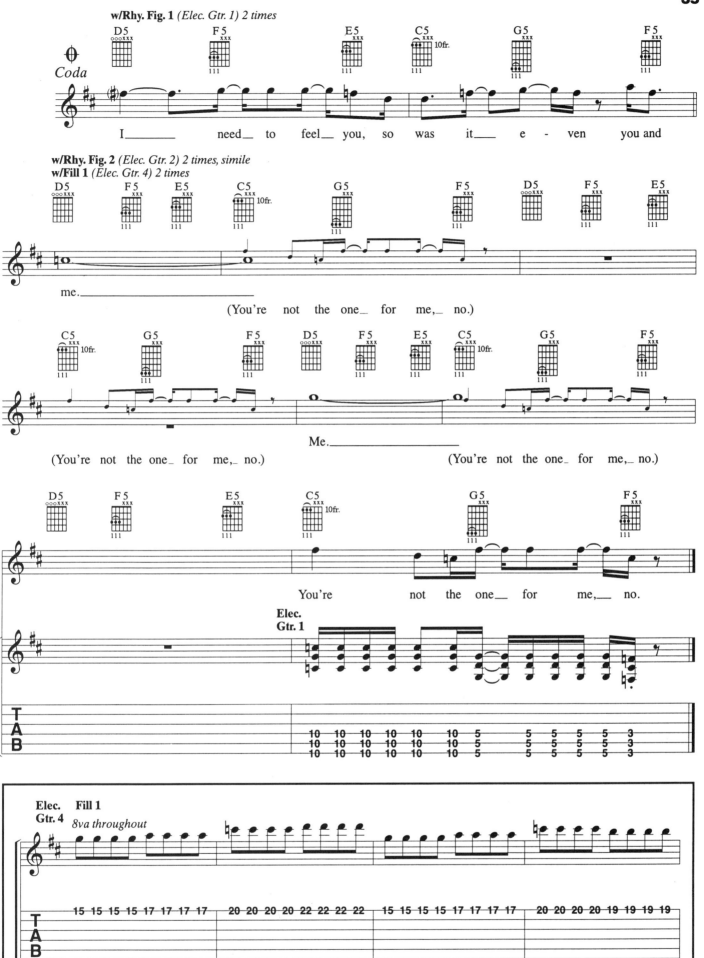

Crawling In The Dark

Words And Music By Douglas Robb And Daniel Estrin

All gtrs. w/Open E tuning:
E-B-E-G#-B-E

⑥ = E   ③ = G#
⑤ = B   ② = B
④ = E   ① = E

Moderate rock ♩ = 92

Intro:
N.C.

Gtr. 1 *(w/slight dist.)*

mf *w/delay*

P.M. throughout

Gtr. 1 tacet

E5 F#5   E5 F#5 D5   A/C#   A5   E5

Gtr. 2 *(w/dist.)*

f

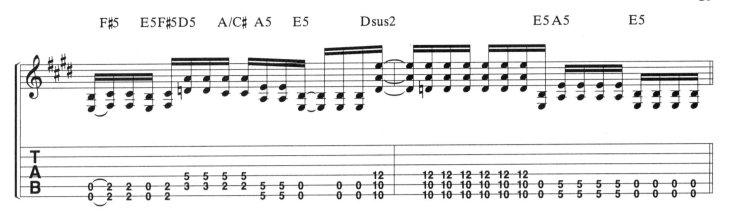

Verse:
Gtr. 2 tacet
N.C.

1. I_____ will__ ded-i - cate__   and sac - ri - fice__ my__ ev - 'ry -
2. Help__ me__ car-ry on__   and show me   it's__ o - kay__ to

Riff A
Gtr. 1

P.M. throughout

thing   for   just   a   sec - ond's_ worth.__   I found my   sto - ry's_ end - ing.
use   my   heart   and not__ my__ eyes___   and nav - i - gate_ the_ dark - ness.

end Riff A

38

w/**Riff A** *(Gtr. 1)*
w/**misc. feedback** *(next 3 meas.)*
w/**Riff B** *(Gtr. 3) 2 times, 2nd time only*

And I_____ wish I could know_ of the di - rec - tions that__ I take_
Will__ the end-ing be___ ev - er com - ing sud - den - ly?_

w/**Fill 1** *(Gtr. 2) 1st time*
w/**Rhy. Fill 1** *(Gtr. 2) 2nd time*

___ and all the choic - es that__ I___ make__ won't end up all__ for noth - ing.
___ Will I ev - er get__ to see___ the end-ing to__ my sto - ry?

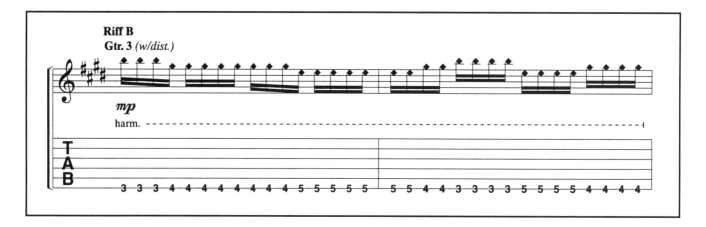

Riff B
Gtr. 3 *(w/dist.)*

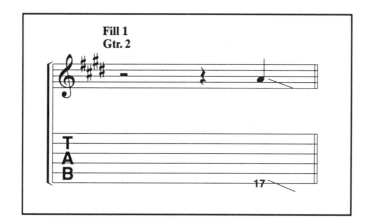

Fill 1
Gtr. 2

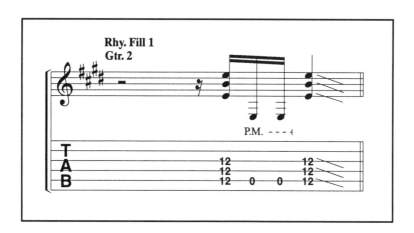

Rhy. Fill 1
Gtr. 2

Chorus:
Gtr. 1 tacet
2nd time, Gtr. 3 tacet

Show__ me__ what it's for.__   Make__ me__ un-der-stand__ it.

Double-time feel   **end Double-time feel**

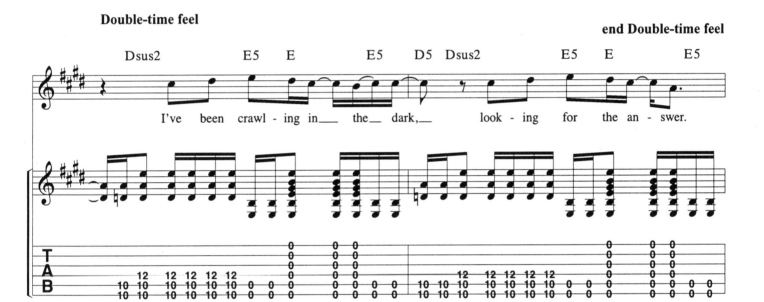

I've been crawl-ing in__ the__ dark,__   look-ing for the an-swer.

3rd time, Double-time feel

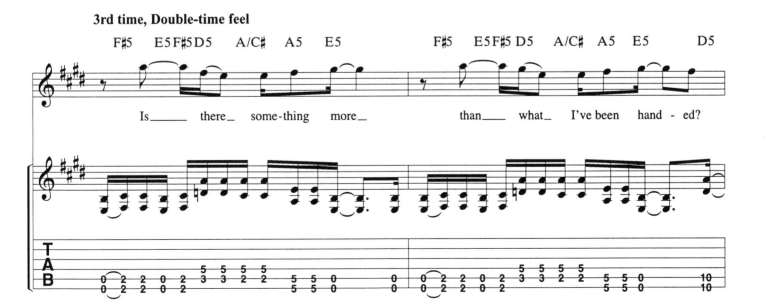

Is_____ there__ some-thing more__   than_____ what__ I've been hand-ed?

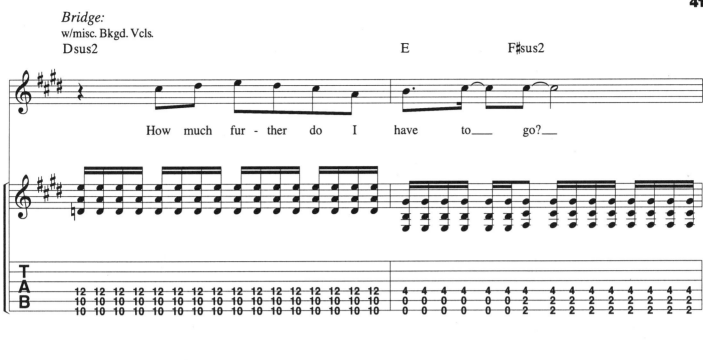

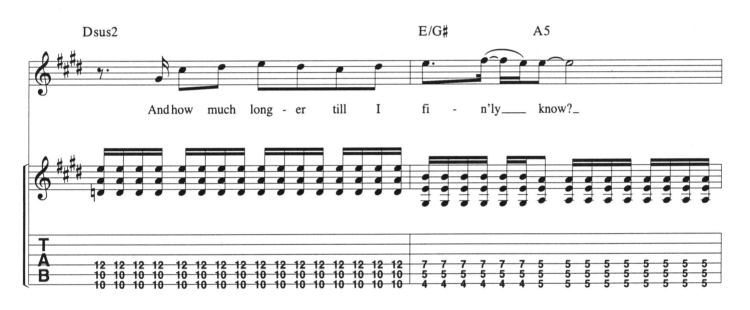

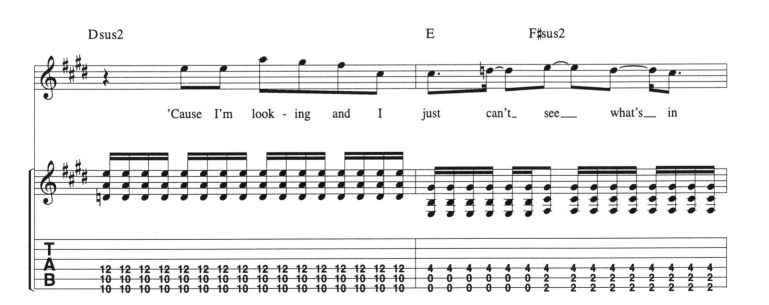

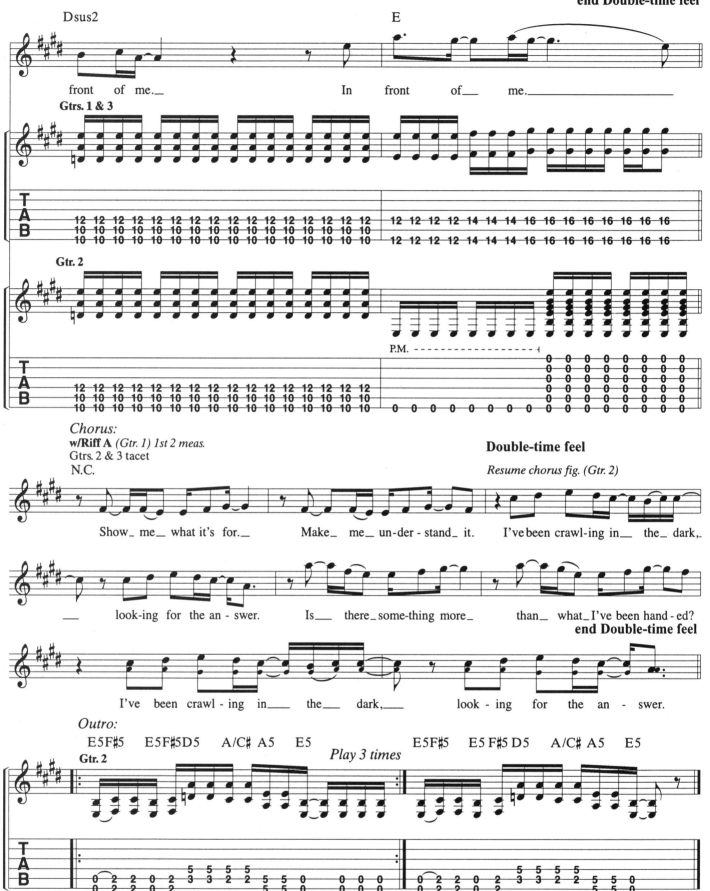

Drive

Words And Music By Brandon Boyd, Michael Einziger, Alex Katunich, Jose Pasillas Ii And Chris Kilmore

Pre-Chorus

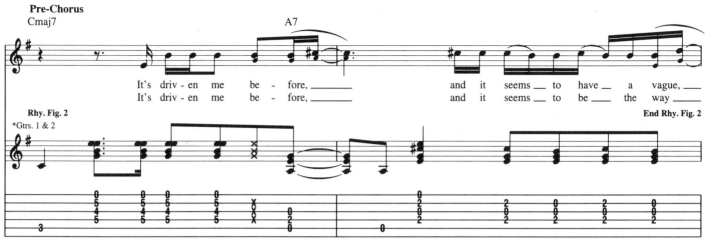

*Composite arrangement.

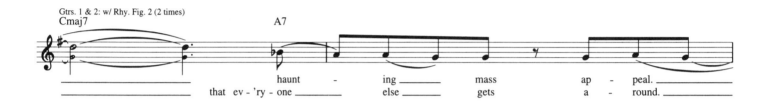

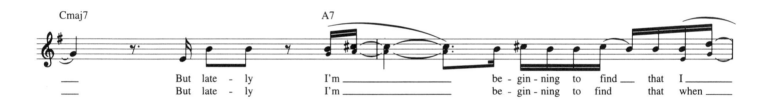

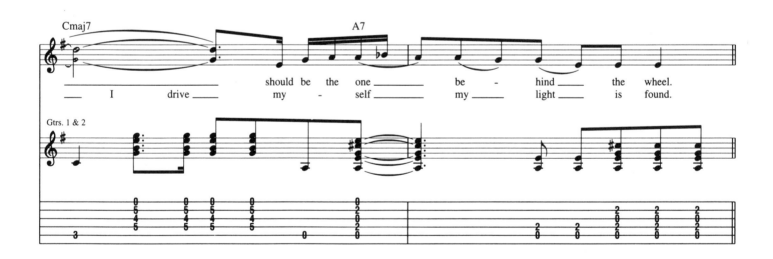

Chorus

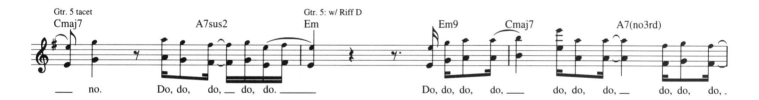

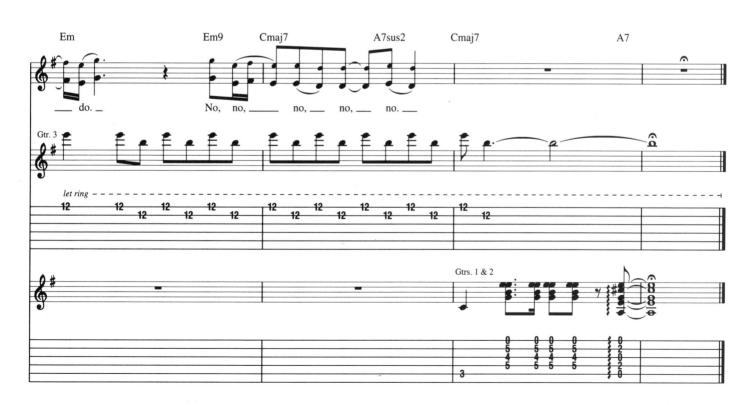

The Fake Sound Of Progress

Words And Music By Michael Chiplin, Lee Gaze, Michael Lewis, Richard Oliver, Stuart Richardson And Ian Watkins

52

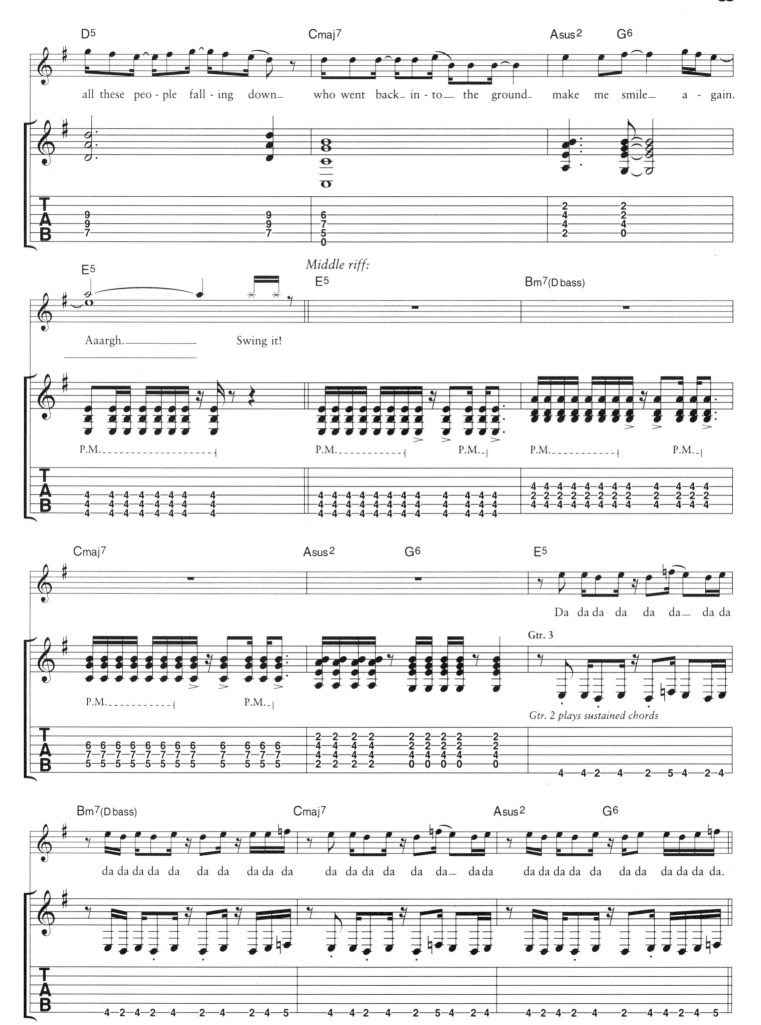

Bridge:

Fat Lip

Words And Music By Greig Nori, Deryck Whibley, Steve Jocz And Dave Baksh

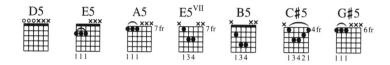

* Composite arrangement

* Doubled throughout

1. Storm-ing through the par-ty like my name was El Ni - ño
2. *See additional lyrics*

When I'm hang-ing out, drink-ing in the back of an El Cam-i - no.

As a

* w/ delay repeats.

Outro

Additional Lyrics

2. Because you don't
   Know us at all, we laugh when old people fall.
   But what would you expect with a conscience so small?
   Heavy Metal and mullets, it's how we were raised.
   Maiden and Priest were the gods that we praised.

2nd Pre-Chorus:
'Cause we like having fun at other people's expense and
Cutting people down is just a minor offense then.
It's none of your concern, I guess I'll never learn.
I'm sick of being told to wait my turn.
I don't want to...

Higher

Words And Music By Scott Tremonti And Mark Tremonti

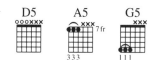

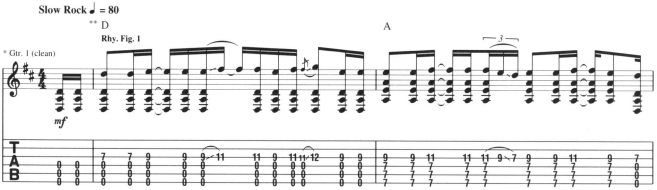

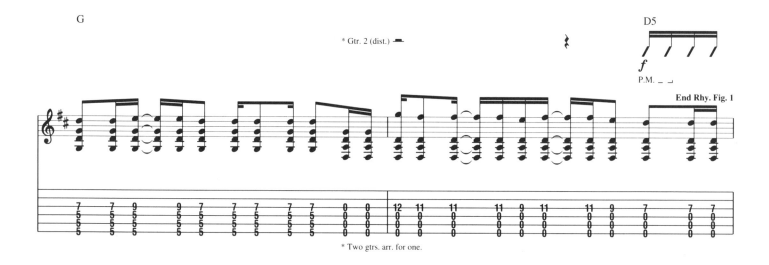

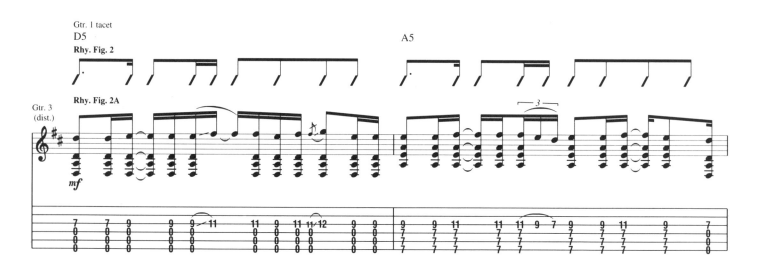

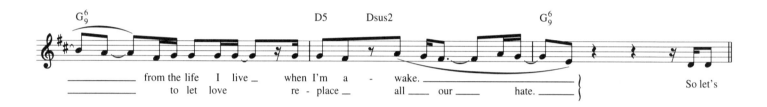

Pre-Chorus

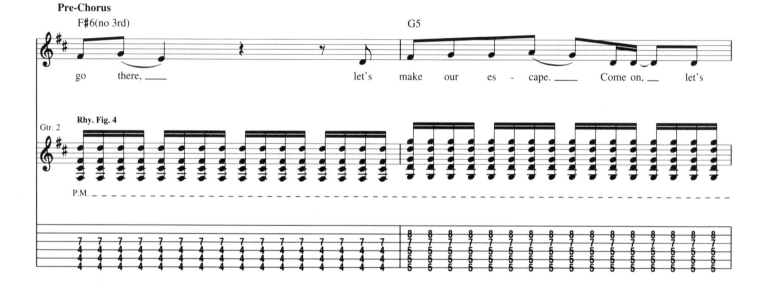

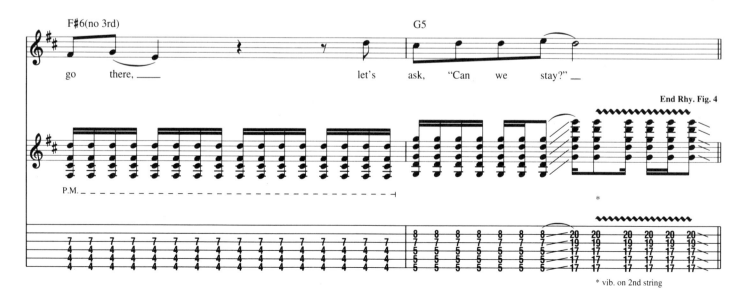

* vib. on 2nd string

How You Remind Me

Words And Music By Chad Kroeger, Michael Kroeger, Ryan Peake And Ryan Vikedal

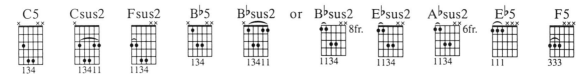

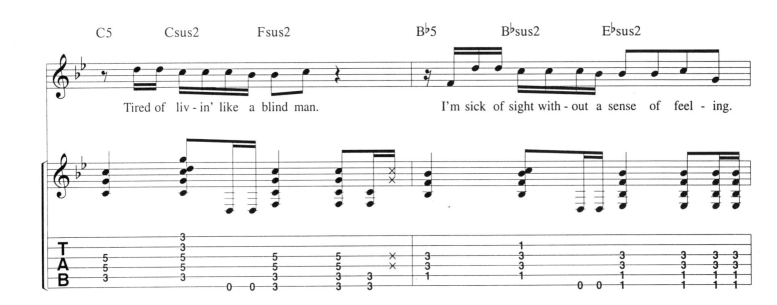

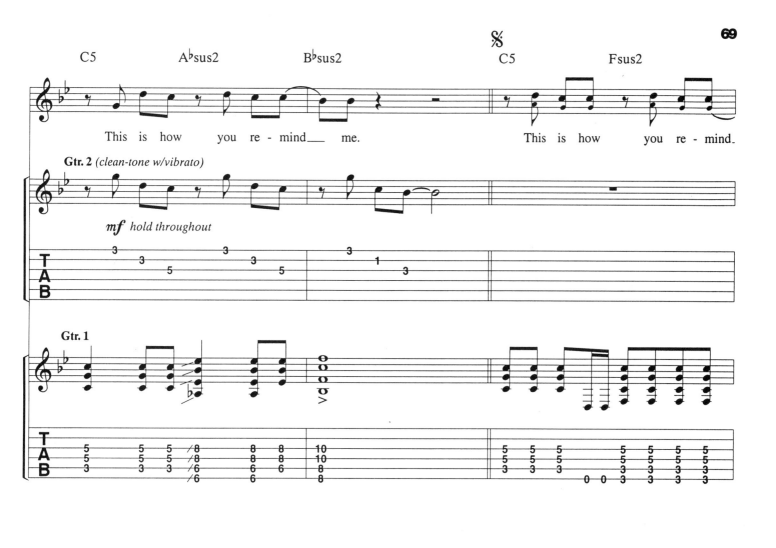

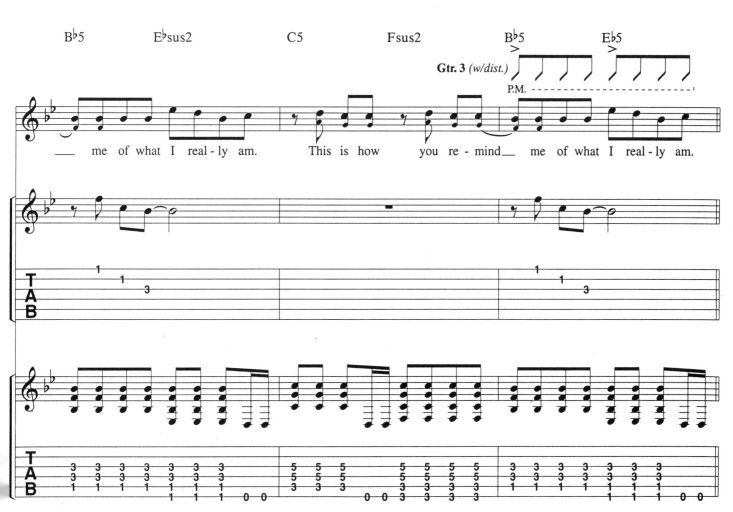

Chorus:

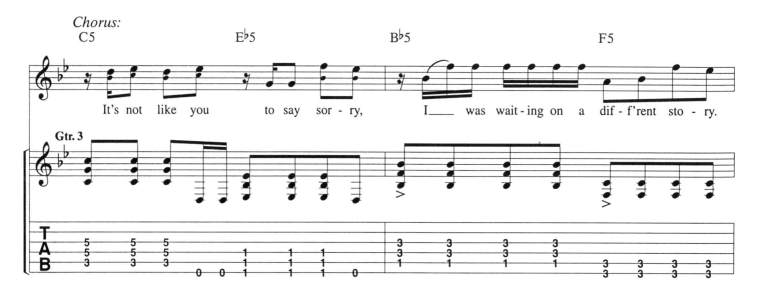

It's not like you to say sor - ry, I___ was wait-ing on a dif - f'rent sto - ry.

Play slash chord on D.S. only.

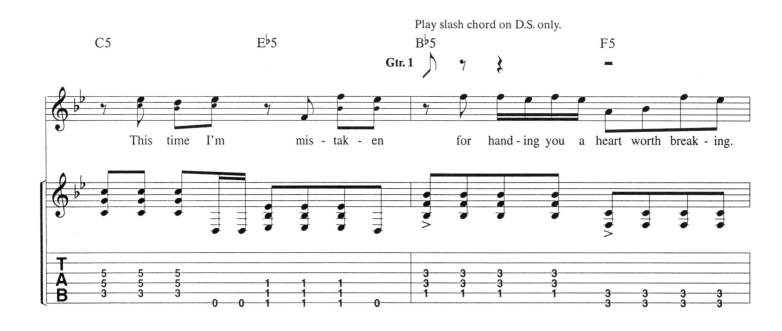

This time I'm mis - tak - en for hand - ing you a heart worth break - ing.

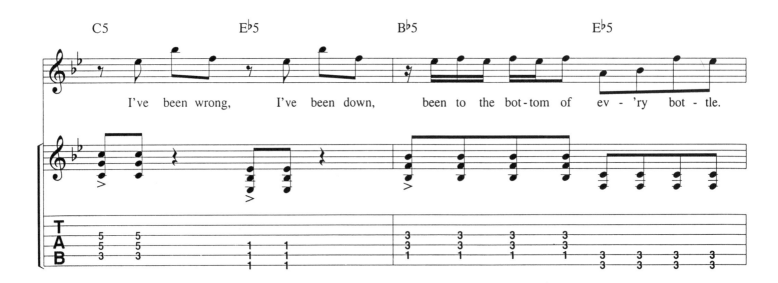

I've been wrong, I've been down, been to the bot-tom of ev - 'ry bot - tle.

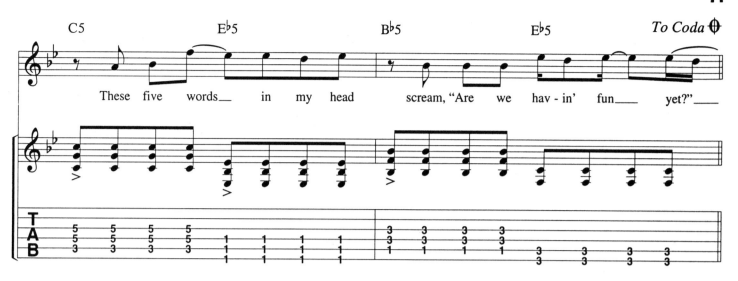

To Coda ⊕

These five words___ in my head scream, "Are we hav - in' fun___ yet?"___

Gtr. 3

Yeah,_ yeah,_ yeah,_ no,__ no. Yeah,_ yeah,_

Gtr. 2

yeah,_ no,__ no. Yeah,_ yeah,_ yeah,_ no,__ no.

Verse 2:
It's not like you didn't know that.
I said I love you and I swear I still do.
And it must have been so bad.
'Cause livin' with me must have damn near killed you.

This is how you remind me of what I really am.
This is how you remind me of what I really am.
(To Chorus:)

In The End

Words And Music By Rob Bourdon, Mike Shinoda,
Bradford Delson, Joe Hahn And Chester Bennington

*Sung 1st & 2nd times only.

It's Been Awhile

Words And Music By Michael Mushok, Aaron Lewis, John April And Jonathan Wysocki

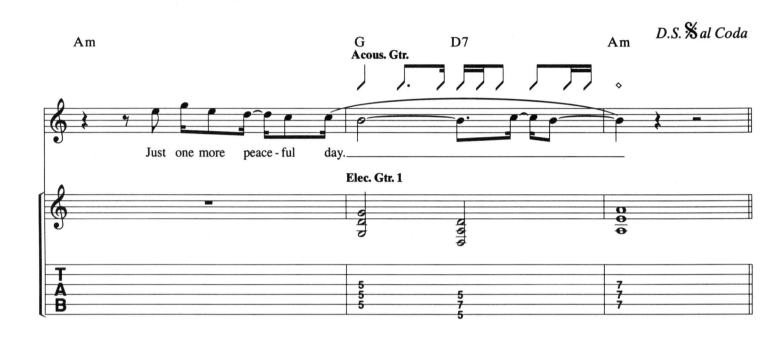

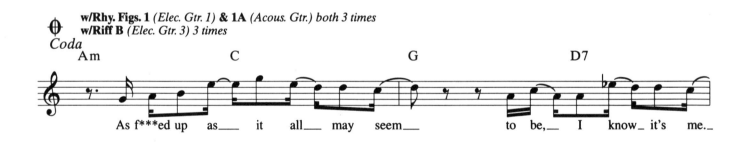

hold_ my hand_ up high.__ And it's been a - while_ since I__ said I'm sor - ry.

Verse 3:
And it's been awhile since I could
Look at myself straight.
And it's been awhile
Since I said I'm sorry.
And it's been awhile since
I've seen the way
Candles light your face.
And it's been awhile, but I can
Still remember just the way you taste.
(To Chorus:)

In Too Deep

Words And Music By Greig Nori And Deryck Whibley

Chorus

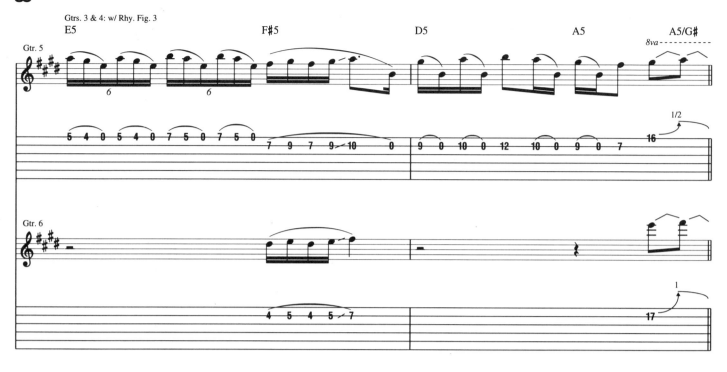

Bridge

I can't sit back and __ won-der why. __ It took so long for __ this to die. __

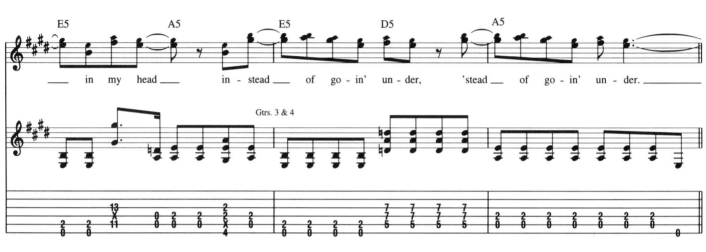

Outro

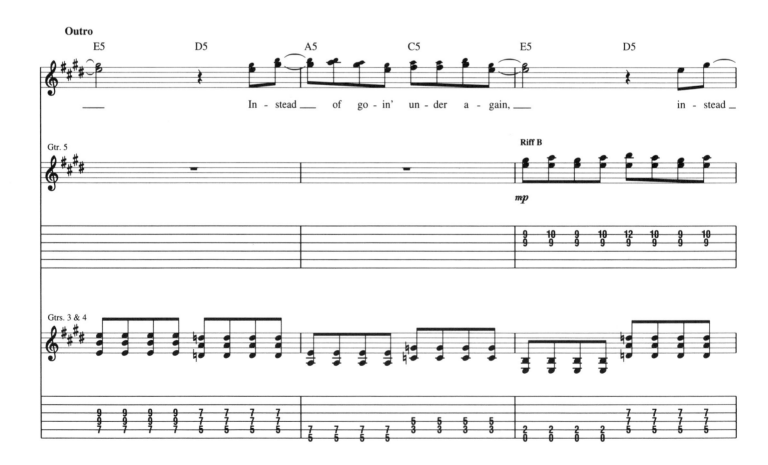

Left Behind

Words And Music By Michael Crahan, Paul Gray, Nathan Jordison And Corey Taylor

96

98

Middle

Words And Music By James Adkins, Thomas Linton, Richard Burch And Zachary Lind

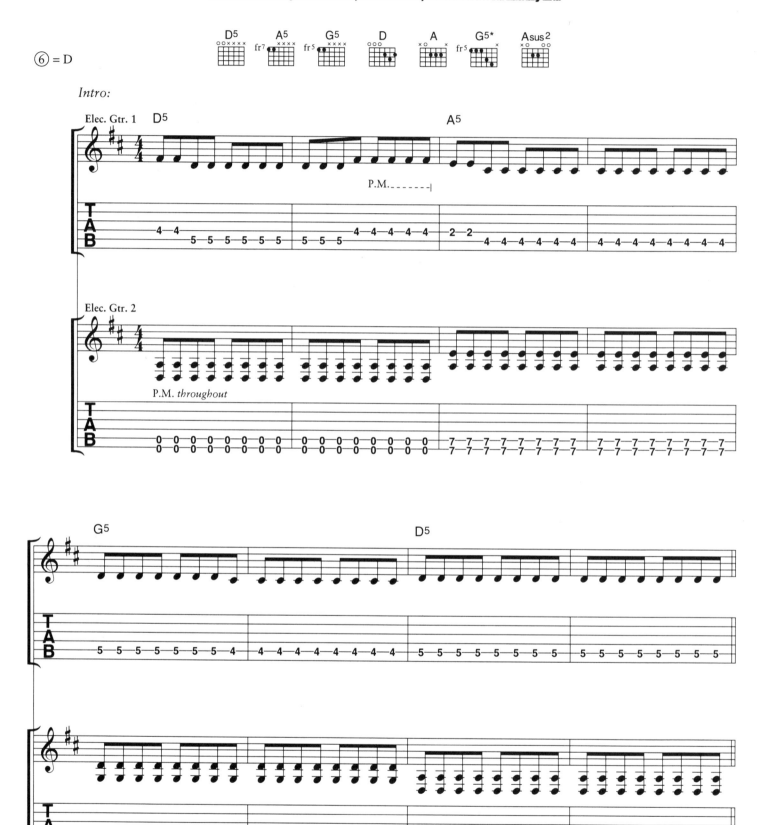

Cherry Lane Music Publishing, New York, NY 10036, USA

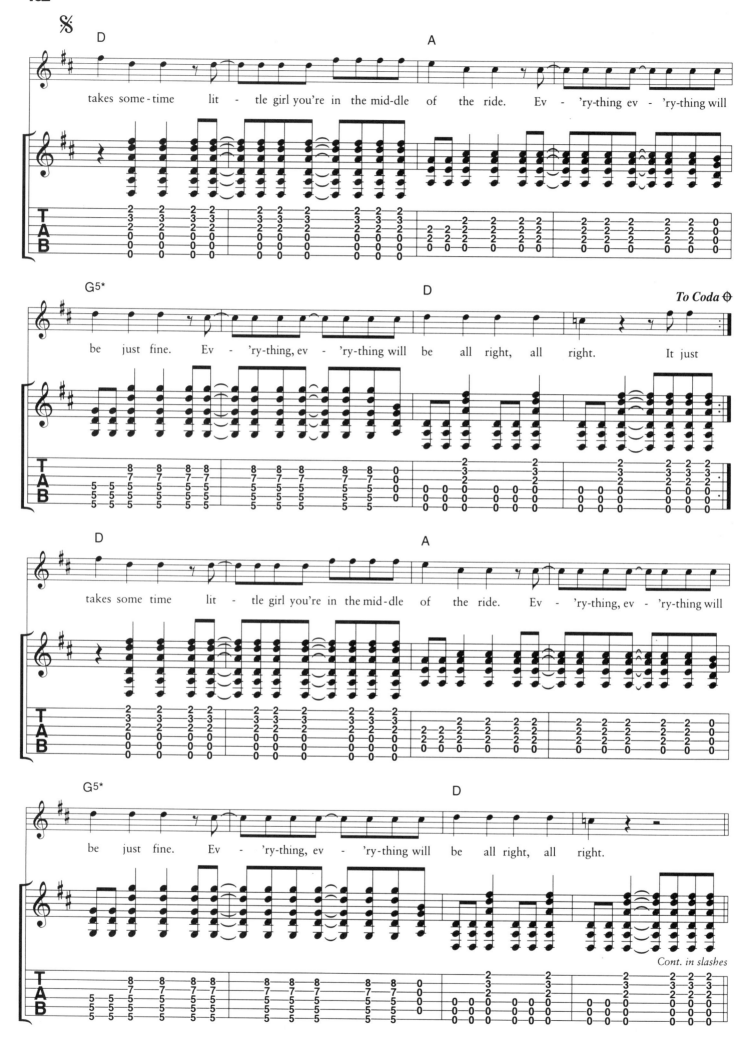

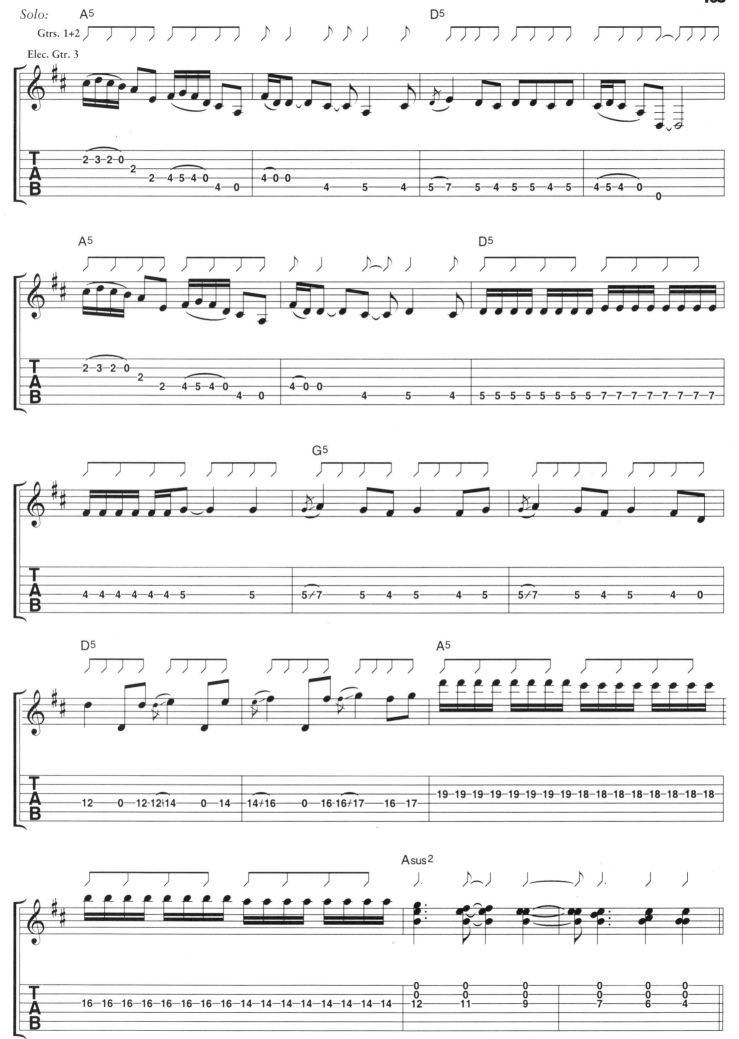

Movies

Words And Music By Terence Corso, Michael Cosgrove, Dryden Mitchell And Tye Zamora

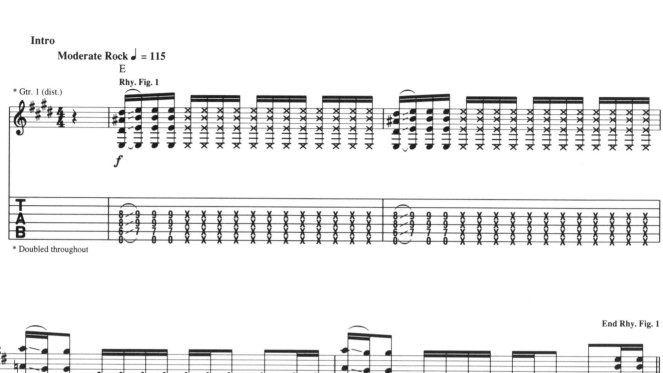

* Chord symbols reflect overall harmony.

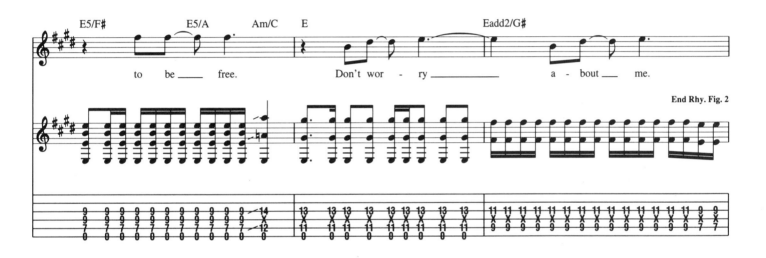

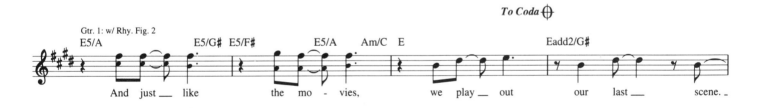

er. ___ In win - ter, ___ we can ___ taste ___ the pain. ___

Bridge

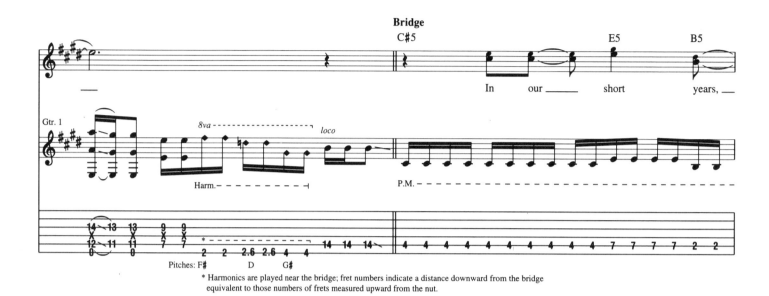

In our _____ short years, ___

Gtr. 1

8va ------- loco

Harm. ------

P.M. ------

Pitches: F#   D   G#

* Harmonics are played near the bridge; fret numbers indicate a distance downward from the bridge equivalent to those numbers of frets measured upward from the nut.

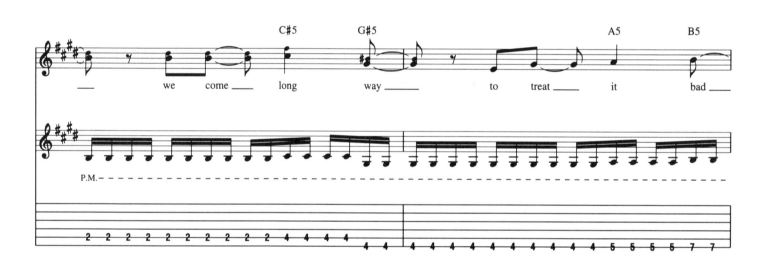

we come ___ long way ___ to treat ___ it bad ___

P.M. ------

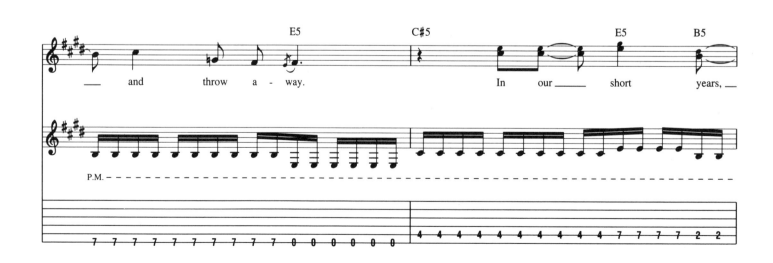

and throw a - way. In our _____ short years, ___

P.M. ------

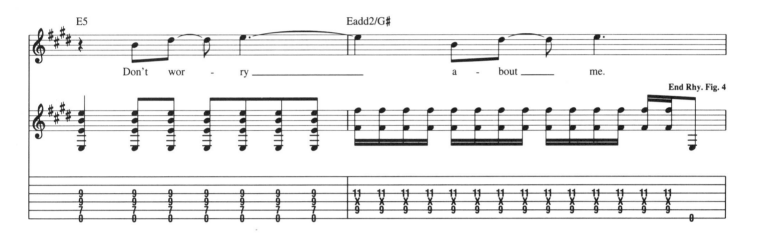

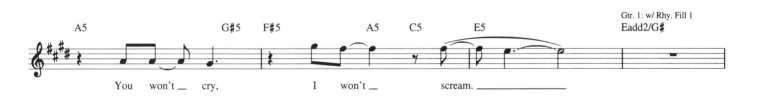

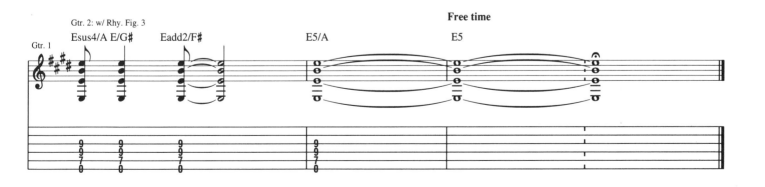

Nothing

Words And Music By Adam Perry, Giles Perry, Mark Chapman, Daniel Carter And Jason Perry

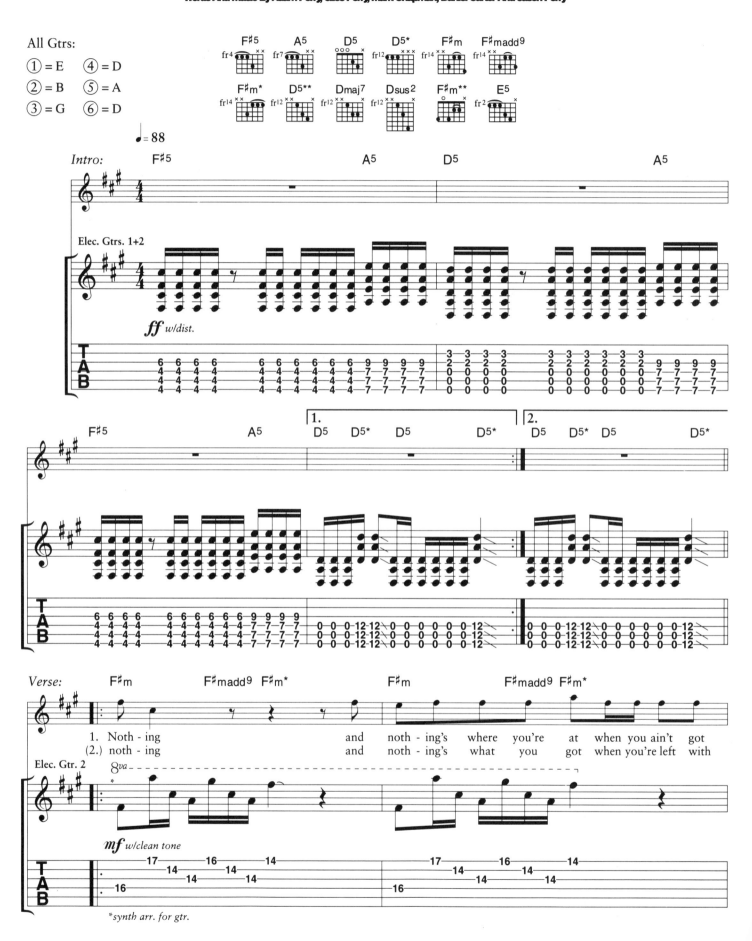

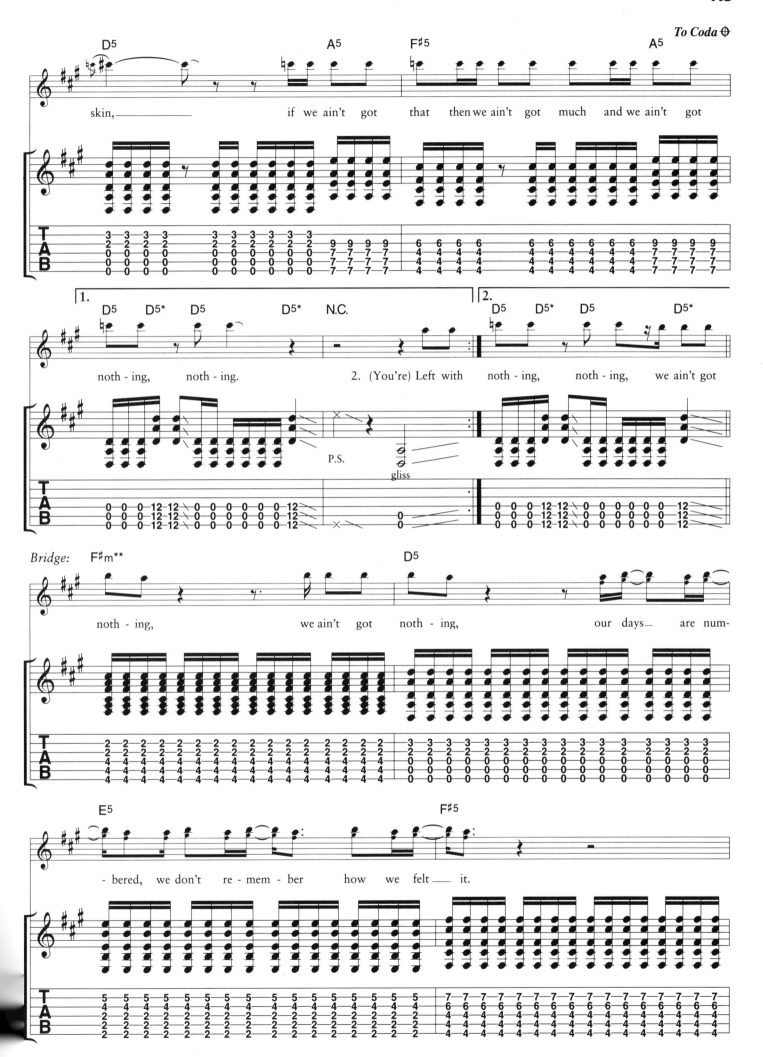

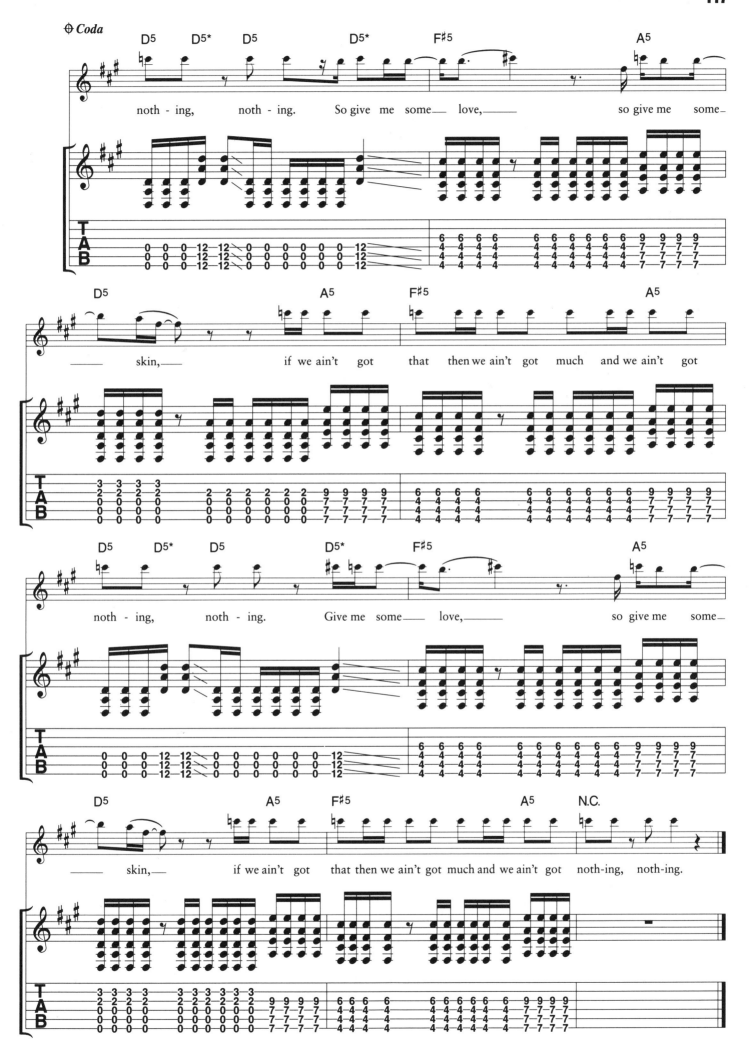

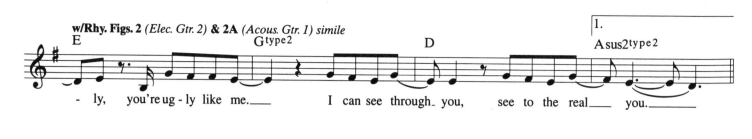

w/Rhy. Figs. **2** *(Elec. Gtr. 2)* **& 2A** *(Acous. Gtr. 1) simile*

- ly, you're ug-ly like me.___ I can see through_ you, see to the real___ you.___

Interlude:

2. All the times_ ___ you.___

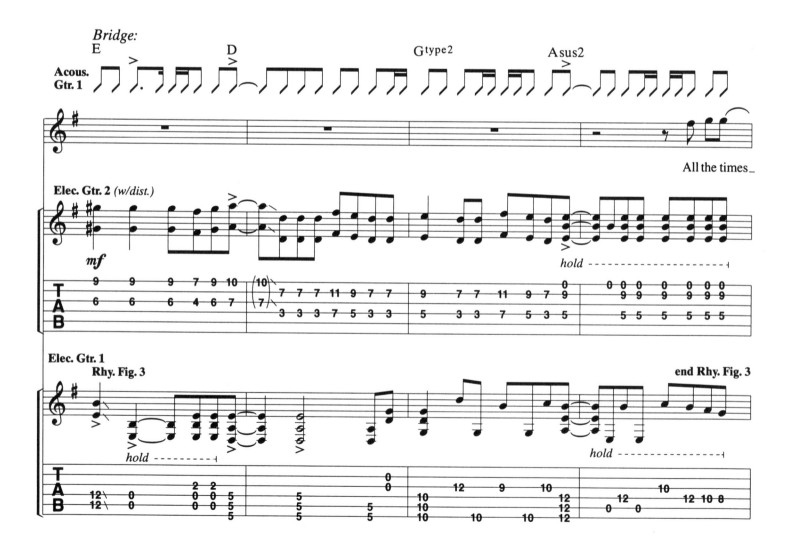

Bridge:

All the times_

Last Resort

Words And Music By Tobin Esperance, Jerry Horton Jr, Jacoby Shaddix And David Buckner

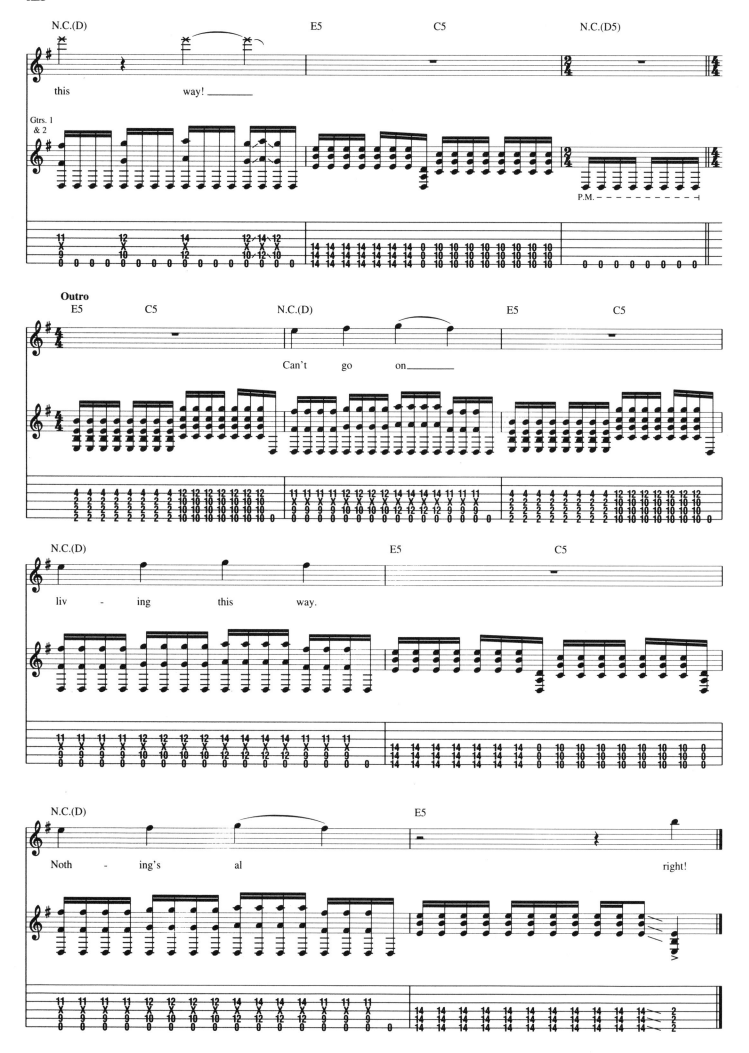

Pardon Me

Words And Music By Brandon Boyd, Michael Einziger, Alex Katunich, Jose Pasillas Ii And Chris Kilmore

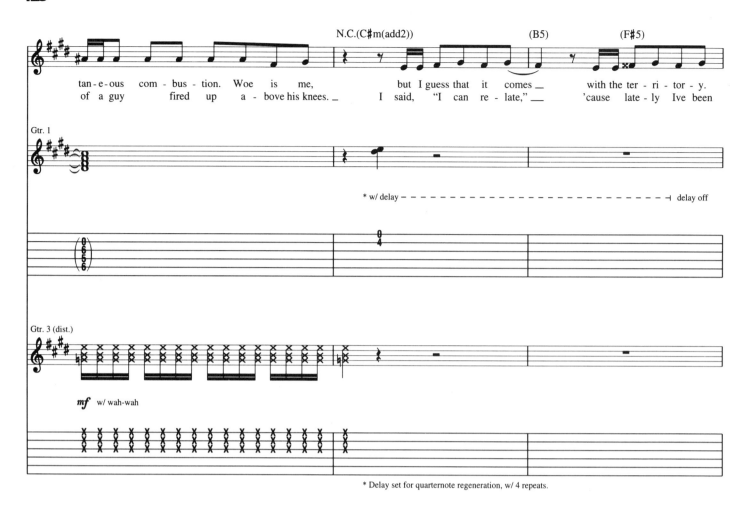

* Delay set for quarternote regeneration, w/ 4 repeats.

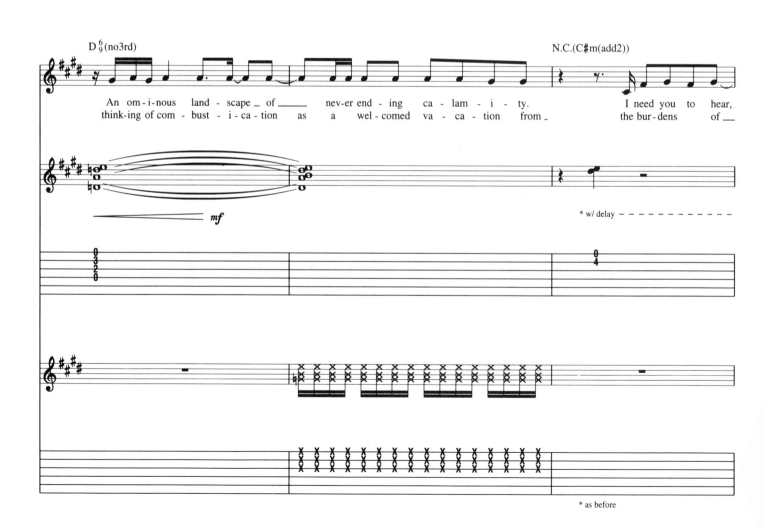

* as before

130

The Rock Show

Words And Music By Mark Hoppus, Tom Delonge And Travis Barker

* Chord symbols reflect basic harmony.

EMI Music Publishing Ltd, London WC2H 0QY

I could-n't wait for the sum-mer and the Warped Tour. I re-mem-ber it's the

Interlude
Gtrs. 1, 2 & 3: w/ Rhy. Fig. 1 & Riff A (2 times)

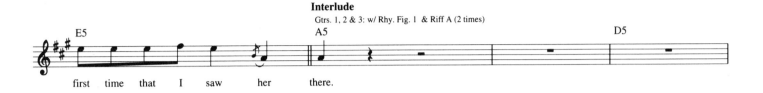

first time that I saw her there.

Verse

2. She's get-tin' kicked out of school 'cause she's fail - ing. I'm kind-a ner-vous 'cause I think all her friends hate me.

She's the one, she'll al - ways be there. She took my hand and that made it I swear be-cause I

% Chorus

{ 1.,3. fell
  2. Fell } in love with the girl at the rock show. She said, "What?" And I told her that I did - n't know.

Sev - en - teen with - out a pur - pose or dir - ec - tion. We don't owe an - y - one a fuck - in' ex - pla - na - tion.

⊕ Coda 1

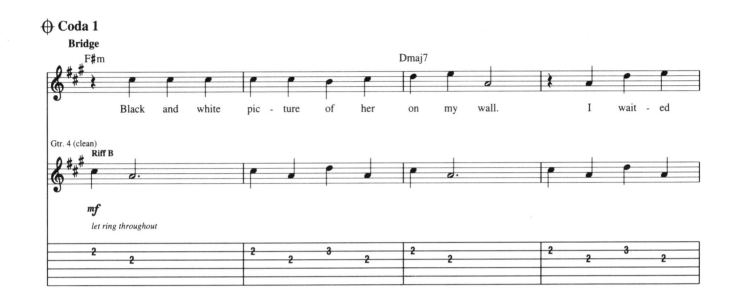

Black and white pic - ture of her on my wall. I wait - ed

for her call. She al - ways kept me wait - ing.

And if I ev - er got an - oth - er chance, I'd still ask

D.S. al Coda 2

her to dance be-cause she kept me wait-ing. I

Coda 2

Outro

Gtrs. 1, 2 & 3: w/ Rhy. Fig. 1 & Riff A (till fade)

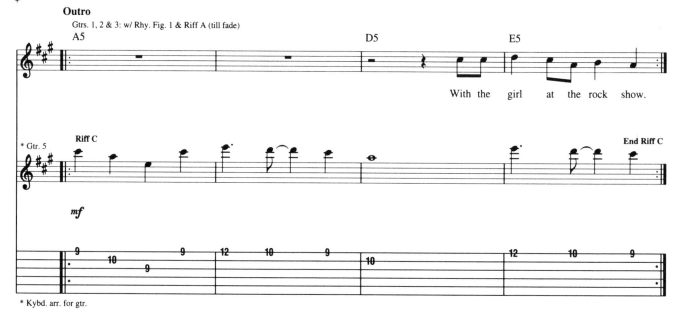

With the girl at the rock show.

Riff C

End Riff C

* Gtr. 5

mf

* Kybd. arr. for gtr.

Gtrs. 4 & 5: w/ Riffs B & C (till fade)

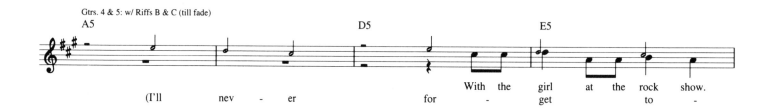

(I'll nev - er for - get at the rock show.

With the girl to -

Play 5 times and fade

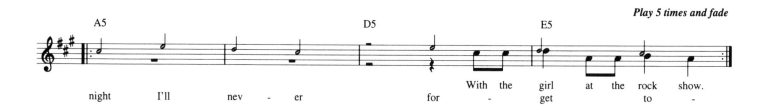

night I'll nev - er for - get to -

With the girl at the rock show.

Rollin'

Words And Music By Wes Borland, Sam Rivers, John Otto, Fred Durst, Leor Dimant And Kaseem Dean

Verses 1 & 2:

Sub. w/Fill 1 *(Elec. Gtr. 3) 1st time only*

Em

know you'll be lov-in' this shit right here, I. and P.__ Biz - kit is right here.
mess with Limp Biz-kit, you can't mess with Limp Biz-kit. Be-cause we get it on ev-'ry day and ev-'ry night. And this

Elec. Gtr. 3 **Riff B**

mf

P.M.

12 12 12   14 14 14   12 12 12   15 15 15 14 14 12 15   12   12   (12)   12

w/Riff B *(Elec. Gtr. 3) 3 times*

Peo-ple in the house put them hands in the air 'cause if you don't care,_ then we don't care._ Yeah!
plat-i-num thing right here, yo, we're doin' it all the time. So you bet-ter get some bet - ter beats and get some bet -ter rhymes.

One, two, three times two, to the six, Jones-in' for your fix of that Limp Biz - kit mix. So
We got the gang set, so don't com - plain yet. Twen - ty-four - sev-en nev-er beg-gin' for a rain check.

where the f*** you at, punk? Shut the f*** up, and pack the f*** up while we f*** this track up.
Old school sol - diers blast-in' out the hot shit, that rock shit put-tin bounce in the mosh pit.

Pre-chorus:

w/Riff A *(Elec. Gtr. 1)*

Em   Bm   Em   Bm

Put   your hands   up.   Put   your hands   up.

Em   Bm   Em   Bm

Put   your hands up.   Put your hands   up.   Put   your hands   up.   I move in,_

Fill 1
Elec. Gtr. 3

P.M.

10 10 7 10

Rollin' (Air Raid Vehicle) - 5 - 4
PGM0039

Shout 2000

Words And Music By Roland Orzabal And Ian Stanley

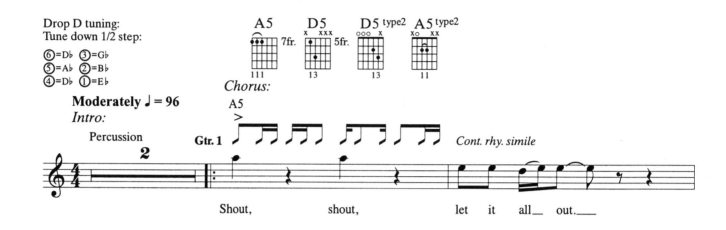

Drop D tuning:
Tune down 1/2 step:
⑥=Db ③=Gb
⑤=Ab ②=Bb
④=Db ①=Eb

Moderately ♩ = 96

Intro:

Percussion

Gtr. 1   *Cont. rhy. simile*

Shout,   shout,   let it all__ out.__

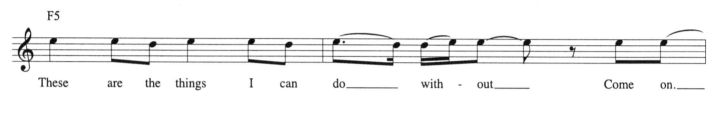

These   are   the   things   I   can   do____   with - out____   Come on.__

__   *(Come   get it on,   come   get it on.)

I'm   talk - ing   to you,___   so come   on.__

*Backing vocals, second time only.

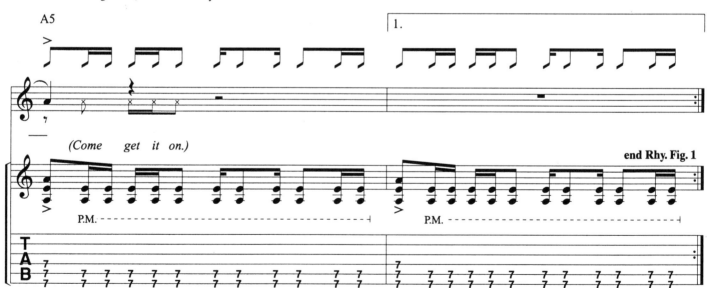

(Come   get   it   on.)

end Rhy. Fig. 1

P.M. -   P.M. -

*Implied harmony.

148

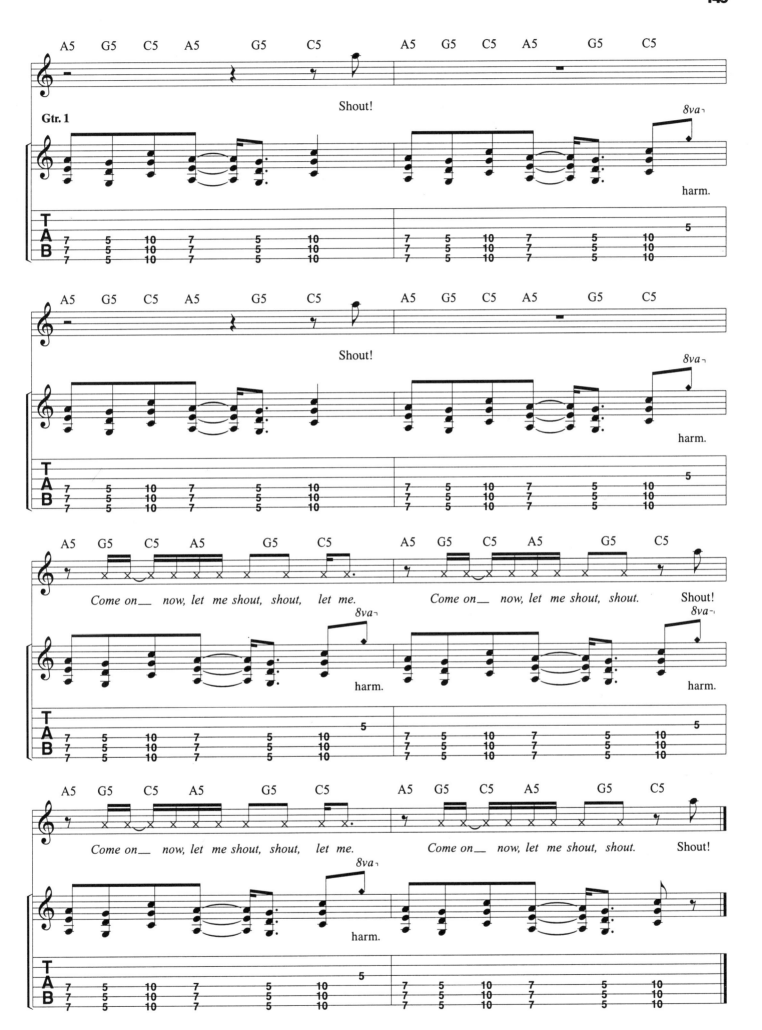

Smooth Criminal

Words And Music By Michael Jackson

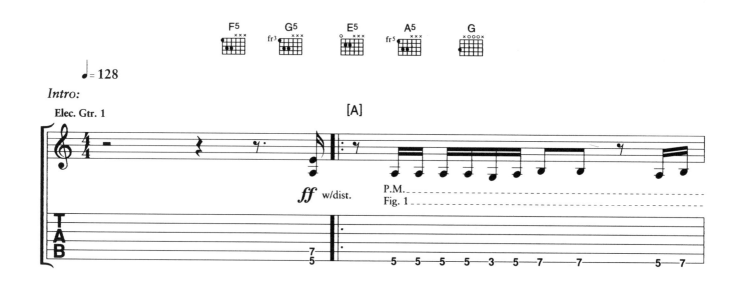

1. As he came in through the win-dow it was the sound of a cre-scen-do.

© 1987 Mijac Music, USA
Warner Chappell Music Ltd, London W6 8BS

You've been hit by, you've been struck by a smooth cri-mi-nal.

156

Tainted Love

Words And Music By Ed Cobb

Too Bad

Words And Music By Chad Kroeger, Michael Kroeger, Ryan Peake And Ryan Vikedal

All gtrs. tune down one whole step w/Drop D tuning:

⑥ = C   ③ = F
⑤ = G   ② = A
④ = C   ① = D

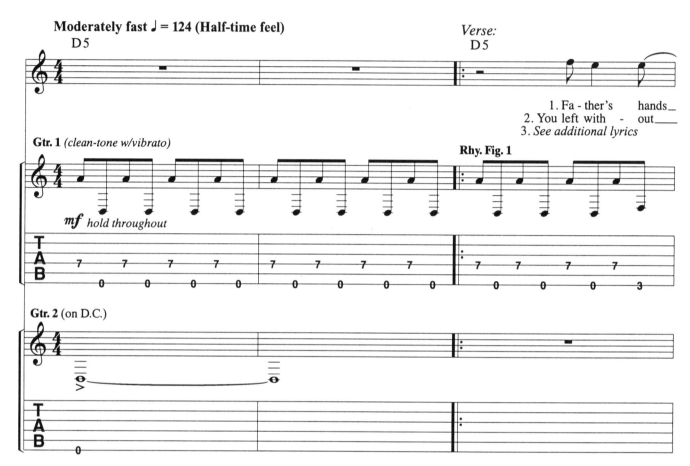

*Composite arrangement.

Chorus:

___ it's stu - pid, too late,___ so wrong,_ so long.___

Rhy. Fig. 2

It's too bad___ we had___ no time_ to re - wind__ let's walk, let's talk..

end Rhy. Fig. 2

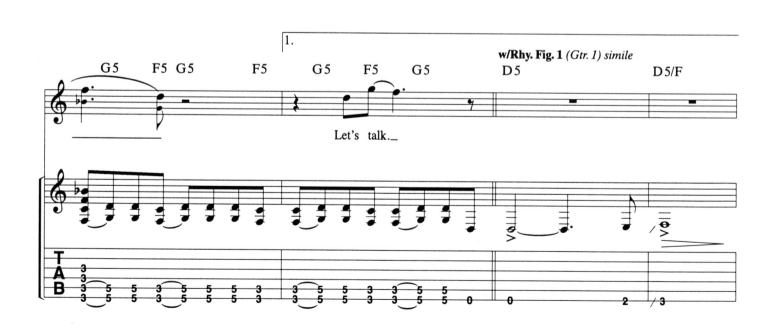

Let's talk._

*Guitars recorded backwards or
played w/whammy pedal effect.

*Implied harmony.

Verse 3:
Father's hands are lined with guilt from tearing us apart.
Guess it turned out in the end, just look at where we are.
We made it out, we still got clothing on our backs
And now I scream about it and how it's so bad,
It's so bad, it's so bad.
(To Chorus:)

Voices

Drop D tuning:
Tune down 1/2 step:

⑥=D♭ ③=G♭
⑤=A♭ ②=B♭
④=D♭ ①=E♭

Words And Music By Mike Wengren, Dan Donegan, David Draiman And Steve Kmak

Moderately ♩ = 110

Intro:

So,

are you breath - ing?   So,

are you breath - ing?   No!   No!

172

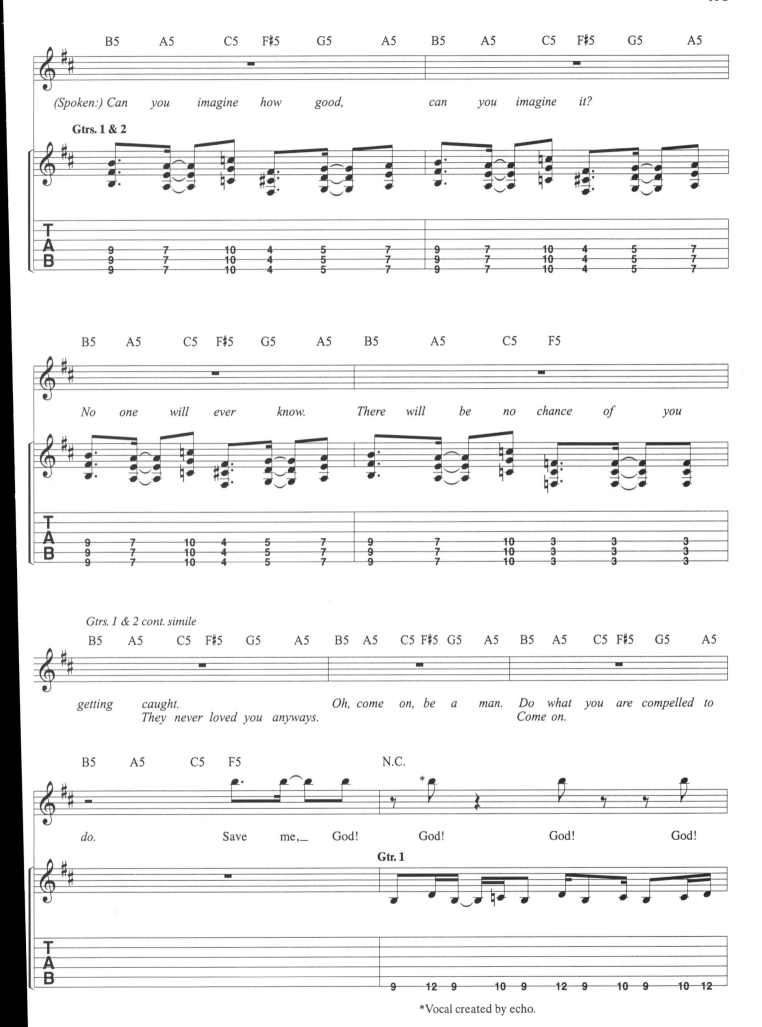

*Vocal created by echo.

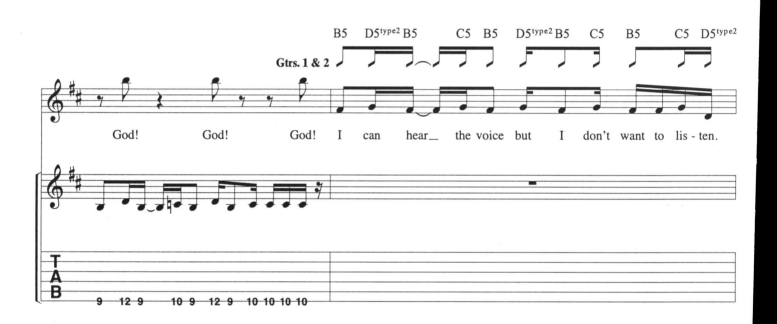

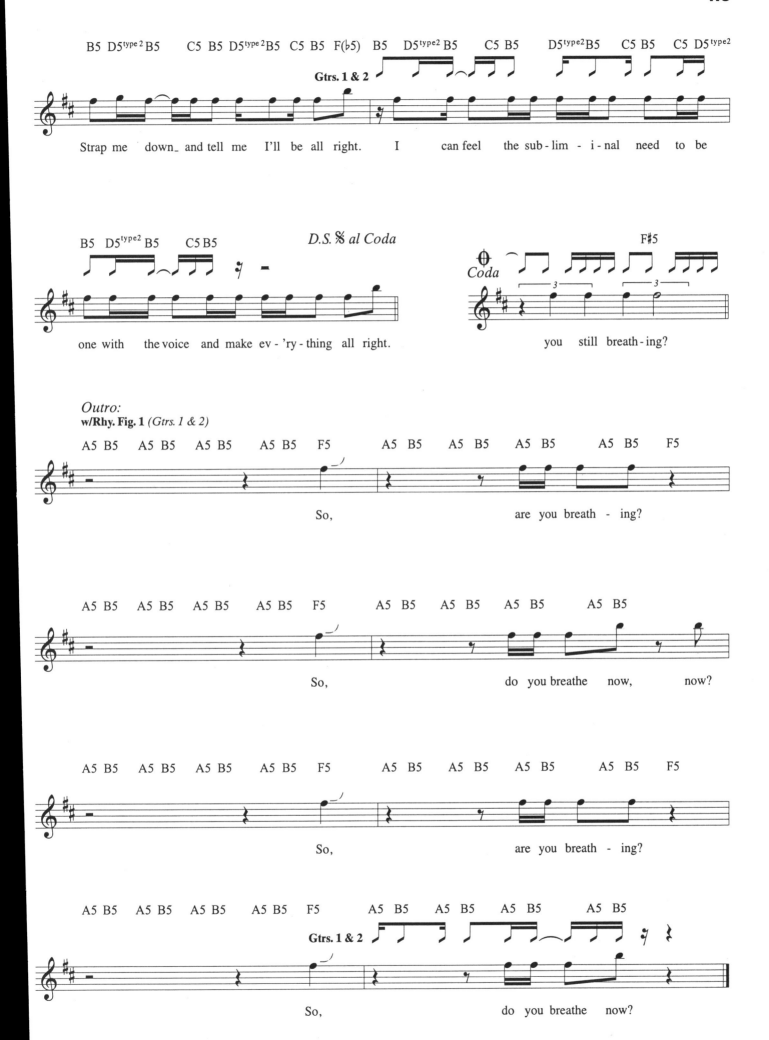

Wait & Bleed

Words And Music By Michael Crahan, Paul Gray, Nathan Jordison And Corey Taylor

178

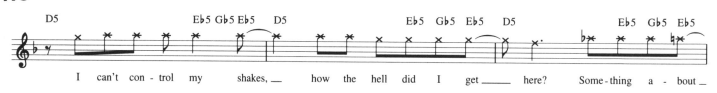

I can't con - trol my shakes, __ how the hell did I get ____ here? Some-thing a - bout __

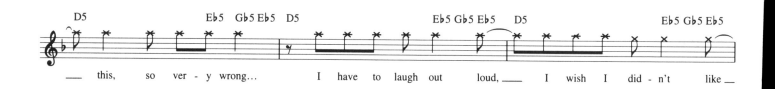

__ this, so ver - y wrong... I have to laugh out loud, __ I wish I did - n't like __

𝄋 Chorus
Gtr. 1: w/ Riff A, 2 times
Gtr. 2: w/ Riff B, 2 times

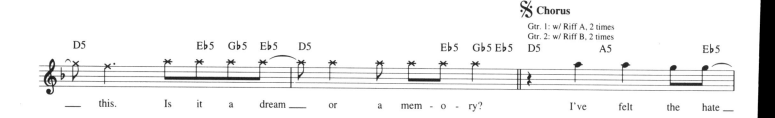

__ this. Is it a dream __ or a mem - o - ry? I've felt the hate __

__ rise up __ in me... __ Kneel down and clear __ the stone __ of leaves... _ I wan - der out __

To Coda ⊕

__ where you __ can't see... __ In - side my shell. __ I wait __ and bleed....

2. Get out - ta my

Gtrs. 1 & 2

Verse
Gtrs. 1 & 2: w/ Rhy. Fig. 1, 4 times

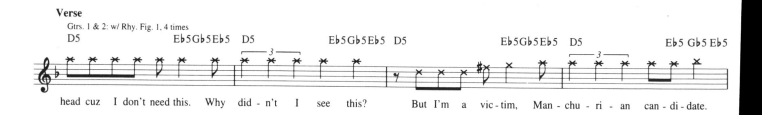

head cuz I don't need this. Why did - n't I see this? But I'm a vic - tim, Man - chu - ri - an can - di - date.

Wish You Were Here

Words And Music By Brandon Boyd, Michael Einziger, Alex Katunich, Jose Pasillas Ii And Chris Kilmore

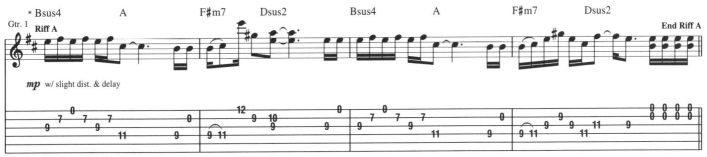

*Chord symbols reflect overall harmony.

Verse

1. I dig ___ my toes ___ in - to ___ the sand. ___
2. I lay ___ my head ___ on to ___ the sand. ___

The o - cean looks _ like a thou - sand dia - monds ___ strewn a - cross ___ a blue plane.
The sky ___ re - sem - bles a back - lit can - o - py _____ with holes ___ punched in it.

I lean ___ a - gainst ___ the wind, ___ pre - tend - in' I ___ am weight - less.
I'm count - ing U. ___ F. O.'s. ___ I sig - nal them with, ___ through my lad - der,

And { in ___ this mo - ment, I ___ am hap - py, _____ hap - py.
that {

𝄋 Chorus

I _____ wish you were here. ___ I _____

yeah, _____ oh. _____

Bridge

The world's _ a rol - ler coast - er, and I ____ am not _ strapped in. ____

Gtr. 1: w/ Rhy. Fig. 1
Gtr. 4 tacet

D.S. al Coda

Coda

Gtrs. 1 & 2: w/ Rhy. Fig. 2

Gtr. 3: w/ Rhy. Fig. 3

Available Now

694A

Take Off Your Pants And Jacket

9504A

DISTURBED
THE SICKNESS

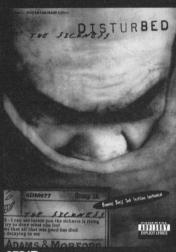
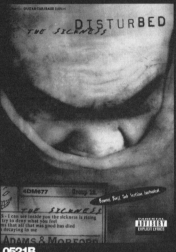

0521B

incubus Make Yourself

HL00690457

---

incubus Morning View

00690544

NICKELBACK
SILVER SIDE UP

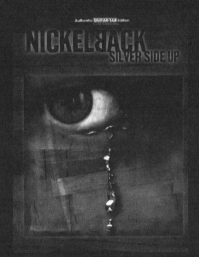

0608B

PUDDLE OF MUDD
come clean

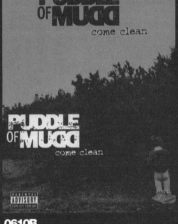

0610B

Slipknot

HL00690530

Slipknot

7A

STAIND
BREAK THE CYCLE

PGM0114

SUM 41
All Killer No Filler

HL00690519

MGA01

Available Now

In all good music shops

Modern Guitar Anthems Blue Book

Thirty songs arranged for Guitar Tablature Vocal.

Starsailor/TheDandyWarhols/ Elbow/Feeder/TurinBrakes/ VexRed//TheElectricSoftParade/ TheWhiteStripes/Radiohead/ BlackRebellMotorcycleClub/ MercuryRev/Haven/TheCoral/ HundredReasons/A/TheMusic/ Doves/MullHistoricalSociety/ TheCooperTempleClause/Idlewild

International Music Publications Limited